GET ACTIVATED

How to shift from instinctive reactions

to intentional responses

ROBIN PULLEN

Get Activated

GET ACTIVATED

How to shift from instinctive reactions to intentional responses

Copyright © Robin Pullen 2019

First published by KDP, Amazon 2019

Self-Improvement, Self-Awareness, Personal Growth, Personal Mastery, Entrepreneurial Development, Business Growth.

For permissions, coaching and training requests, speaking inquiries and bulk order purchase options email us at getactivated@robinpullen.com.

ISBN 978-0-6399427-0-4 | the printed book version
ISBN 978-0-6399427-1-1 | the electronic book version
ISBN 978-0-6399427-2-8 | the audiobook version

Cover, layout & typesetting design: Robin Pullen
www.robinpullen.com

Get Activated

All rights reserved except for the quotation of short passages for the purposes of criticism or review. No part of this publication may be reproduced, stored in a retrieval system, copied or transmitted by any means electronic mechanical photocopying or otherwise without the prior written permission of the author and publisher.

NO PROFESSIONAL ADVICE.
This is a work of non-fiction. The information contained in or made available through this book and any related resources cannot replace or substitute for the services of trained professionals in any field including financial, medical, psychological, or legal matters.

The author does not dispense medical advice or prescribe the use of any technique either directly or indirectly as a form of treatment for mental, physical, emotional or medical problems without the professional advice of a physician. The author's intent is only to offer information of a general nature to help you on your quest for personal mastery and wellbeing.

The author and publisher will not be liable for any direct, indirect, consequential, special, exemplary or other damages that may result, including but not limited to economic loss, injury, illness or death. You alone are responsible and accountable for your decisions, actions and results in life, and by your use of the principles, strategies or ideas available in this book, you agree not to attempt to hold us liable for any such decisions, actions or results, at any time, under any circumstance.

Get Activated

Contents

DEDICATION 7
ACKNOWLEDGEMENTS 8
INTRODUCTION 13
WHO IS THIS 15
PROPRIOCEPTION 19
REMIND ME AGAIN, HOW DO I REALLY WORK? 24
UNPACKING THE INSIGHTS 40
UNPACKING YOUR CHEMISTRY 51
GETTING YOUR POWER BACK 62
THE ROLE OF EMOTION 75
LEVERAGING YOUR INSTINCT 82
BECOME BODY CONSCIOUS 87
THE INSTINCT OVER INTENTION TRAP 92
WHAT STATE ARE YOU IN? 98
READY FOR A CHANGE WITHIN 103
THE ACTIVATED INTELLIGENCE TRIFECTA 111
GET ACTIVATED – HABITS OF THE ACTIVATED LIFE 122
THE ART OF LETTING GO 136
LEARNING TO LISTEN TO YOUR BODY 153
THAT ALL THINGS CAN BE RENEWED 172
CONCLUSION 183
ABOUT THE AUTHOR 187

Get Activated

DEDICATION

For the most precious people in my world, my princess Rebecca-Ruth the Kind and Compassionate, and my boys Michael the Mighty, Tyrone the Strong and Seth the Courageous.

May you know something of my heart, my passion and my mission. May this body of knowledge be to you something of a legacy that will empower you to be more than you can imagine. You guys are my most beautiful reason and give me courage to be the best version of me I can be.

For my mom who lives daily in more discomfort and strain than anyone should have to. I often find myself wondering if so much of what you carry is truly yours to bear. Something of the intuitive soul in me breaks as I watch and silently wonder what more can I do. Perhaps in this collection of thoughts some tactics, insights or tools may prove helpful for you to live your best years yet.

ACKNOWLEDGEMENTS

I am grateful for all the opportunities to have trained and coached individuals in cities and towns across the continent. To be able to do that, I have to say a big thank you to the business owners and corporate clients who made it all possible.

Most of all thank you to the individual people who opened their heart towards me as a trainer and coach and let me help them on their journey of personal and professional development. Without you, I would not have had the opportunity to serve so many people and in so doing the chance to develop and improve my experience, expertise and skills.

In the end, the truth is that I have written this book for someone just like me. I hope that you join me on my journey as I set out to make sense of and master these thoughts. That more and more often, just like you I too can learn to live the activated life.

PART ONE

INTRODUCTION

I honestly did not think that I would enjoy the phenomenon that has become CrossFit or functional training and yet I found myself about two years into my journey with surprising discipline and just loving it.

Coach plays a selection of background music during each session. I am clearly getting older as the style I prefer is quite different from that of the rest of the class. But then when I get to make the selection, or better yet when I get to play a track off my phone I often get members of the class come and say how much they enjoyed the session and mention how the music selection had something to do with it.

There are a few tracks that the other guys like to play that somehow just switch me off. It's not that I can't do the exercise or take part in the routine set up for the class. It's just that when that style of music plays I seem to lose my ability to function at my best.

I lose something in my ability to hold my attention. I struggle to keep focus. I struggle to keep timing. I lose the ability to manage my breath and keep the momentum in my movements. It's like when certain songs play I somehow become a weaker version of me.

Yet when it is my song selection, or when the style of music plays that I resonate with, oh my, then I feel like I become totally invincible. That is what this book is about. When you put this book down having finally finished reading through to the end, I want you to know what it feels like to "be invincible".

It's about developing the ability in any given situation to choose an intentional reaction over a natural or instinctive response. In particular, it is about developing the ability to choose a favorable behavior. It's about developing the capacity to consciously select a set of actions that will best match your intention and serve your purpose as you set out to materialize a set of desired outcomes in any given context.

What I want you to discover in the pages that follow is that you have been given the permission and power to choose. Then it is in your hands how you develop this capability into the ability to make a conscious choice that transforms an instinctive or default reaction into a new intention driven and purposeful response.

I don't know about you however sometimes I find myself in a situation when I respond in a way that does not serve my intention or help me get closer to my desired outcomes. I sure didn't plan to behave that way and definitely do not find the consequences to be desirable. It's not like I was thinking about sabotaging myself or that I knew what I was doing. The problem is that I was not actively thinking or remotely aware of what not to do.

WHO IS THIS

And what happened to the real me?

Take a minute to think back to when you could enjoy the results of an intentional response to an event even if you did not set out to choose it. The influence that music has over your behavior like that of my experience in the CrossFit gym is a great example.

Have you ever noticed how one style of music or even a particular song can have such a strong impact over how you feel in your physiology or body. This is most evident to me in a gym. When the 'right' music plays it makes everything feel right. It is almost as if it unlocks an invisible force.

When the right music plays you feel like you are a stronger, better person. You think in a different way and you feel invigorated. Your body responds and behaves in a different way. You feel lighter and stronger and quicker and dare I say almost invincible.

Find yourself in the exact same place, doing the same activities with the same equipment but change the music, and you experience something completely different.

When the 'wrong' kind of music plays it is as if all the wrong re-responses take place. Your thinking changes from positive, powerful and exciting to something negative, destructive and dysfunctional. Your feeling shifts from empowered and invincible to disconnected and weak. Your body seems to lose touch with its energy source. A moment earlier you felt that you could on the world. Suddenly you now feel tired and would rather lie down and sleep.

How is it that something as simple as selecting the music that you listen to can have such a dramatic impact on how your body reacts and the resulting experience that emerges in the environment that you find yourself in?

The first thing to note is that the changes we are talking about are not primarily external or environmental. The transformation we are looking to understand is largely internal. I like to describe it as three domains that you can learn to have more control over.

In each of these domains, there are a set of practices that will help you exercise the influence necessary to unlock a set of particular outcomes that you are looking for in any given situation.

In the arena of corporate training, we often teach our delegates the principle of 'Locus of Control'. Simply put, if you are a person with an internal locus of control you believe that you can influence events and their outcomes. A person with an external locus of control will blame outside forces to have influence over events rendering them the victim of circumstance.

In the words that follow I want to show you that with the appropriate knowledge and understanding you can develop a powerful internal locus of control and exercise intentional influence over outcomes despite the majority of external components that make up events in your particular context.

Remember the sound of the music as you began to exercise? So listen, if it's been a while since you were in a gym just let your imagination work with me a little. Better yet, go and sit in your car for a moment, as if you were going to the gym, and turn on the radio to play some music. If you were with me in my car, sitting comfortably in the passenger seat I would let you select the first song.

Most people would not put much effort into this. Probably only select the familiar local radio station that plays upbeat commercial music that has something with a beat. You might even know most of the words as you begin to sing along. For a moment you feel happy even singing out a loud before you realize that I can hear you too.

Then song changes to an unfamiliar track. It's not that it's a bad song or you that do not like listening to it. It's just that somehow the magic has dissolved and the feeling at the moment completely changes.

I know this feeling all too well in the gym. At the start of a session, I am looking forward to another good workout. Even if I am not in the best mood I made all the effort to get out to the gym. So I have decided to do my best to make the session count. Then I hear the song selection and my energy shifts again. It doesn't matter what I do I just can't seem to get 'into the zone'.

    I try talking myself up back into a positive state. I remind myself that "I can do this". I try visualizing the success of my last workout session. Yet somehow I just can't seem to get myself activated or get back into the zone for the workout.

PROPRIOCEPTION

What is it about the sound that my body reacts to?

ENERGY & VIBRATION

We can better describe sound as vibrations of energy that travel through a medium like the air. The music that you are listening to is energy expressed in waves making up frequencies received and translated through your ears. These advanced and very sensitive organs transmit and interpret sound to the brain.

The sound energy travels through the outer ear into the auditory canal, causing the eardrum to vibrate. This then causes three bones, the hammer, the anvil and the stirrup to move. The vibrations travel through the fluid in the cochlea in the inner ear, stimulating thousands of tiny hair cells. This results in the transformation of the vibrations into electrical impulses which the brain perceives as sound.

CONSCIOUS PROCESSING

When last did you consciously process a sound stimulus you have just heard? Perhaps it was the alarm in the house next door or the crash of a door closing. Did time slow down for you as your mind recognized that it had heard a particular sound?

You do not necessarily register the wave of energy as it arrives on your outer ear and starts a chain reaction that leads all the way through into your inner brain. You do not consciously feel the changes in your body as the electrical impulses are process and translate. You do not notice the release of chemicals which start a horde of hormonal responses that you experience in the form of a physical sensation at nerve points all across your body.

Did you notice your breathing pattern change or the temperature of your skin rise as the sweat glands began to secrete just a touch more heavily than they were a moment ago?

You do not notice the muscles all the way down your spine into your lower back tense up or that your toes have curled up as the sensation of tension and frustration is experienced all across your body until you feel your shoulders pulled up tight.

Or perhaps you hear a set of events and somewhere in the back of your mind you hear your invisible voice say "oh, there's the neighbors alarm going off again."

Now that is quite a complex process we have just described, one we give a little conscious thought or attention to. Yet this kind of process is taking place, and your mind is processing it and thousands like it, hundreds of times every minute.

They do not go without reaction. Your brain has developed complex reactions, both natural and instinctive, most of them 'invisible' to your top of mind attention. The vast majority of them take place unconsciously.

UNCONSCIOUSNESS

While in an awake state you may recognize that these processes are taking place, the significance of many them is unconsciousness to you. It is not enough to be awake and alert if you want to live an activated life.

You will need to learn to become aware and develop your proprioception, a sense of the position and posture of the body and its response to the environment you find yourself in.

> [Activation code] Your brain has developed complex reactions, the vast majority of them which take place unconsciously.

SENSORY & PERCEPTION

Sensation and perception are two separate processes that are very closely related. Sensation is input about the physical world obtained by our sensory receptors, and perception is the process by which the brain selects, organizes, and interprets these sensations. In other words, senses are the physiological basis of perception.

There are five classical human senses: sight, sound, taste, smell, and touch. Two other senses, kinesthesia and the vestibular senses, have also become widely recognized.

Kinesthesia is the perception or sense-making of the positioning of the parts of the body, commonly known as "body awareness." Vestibular senses detect gravity, linear acceleration (like that of speeding up or slowing down on a straight road), and rotary acceleration (speeding up or slowing down around a curve). Both kinesthesia and the vestibular senses help us to regulate our balance.

[Activation code] Senses are the physiological basis of perception.

SENSORY INFORMATION

Sensory information like that of taste, light, odour, pressure, vibration, heat, and pain is perceived through the body's sensory receptors. These sensory receptors include the eyes, ears, mouth, nose, hands, and feet and the skin as a whole.

Rod and cone receptors in the eye's retina perceive light; cilia in the ear perceive sound; chemical receptors in the nasal cavities and mouth perceive smell and taste; and muscle spindles, as well as pressure, vibration, heat and pain receptors in the skin, perceive the many sensations of touch.

Specialized cells in the sensory receptors convert the incoming energy, like that of the sound waves that make up the music we enjoy into neural impulses. These neural impulses enter the cerebral cortex of the brain, which is made up of layers of neurons with many inputs.

These layers of neurons function like mini microprocessors, and it is their job to organize the sensations and interpret them in the process of perception.

Without losing focus on the point of this conversation, what then are those impulses or more importantly how does your brain interpret and respond to them?

> [Activation code] Kinesthesia is the perception or sense making of the positioning of the parts of the body, commonly known as "body awareness."

REMIND ME AGAIN, HOW DO I REALLY WORK?

These mental processes and behaviors are directly controlled by the brain. I don't know about you however I may need a quick visit back to school to get my head around this, or at least some of the fundamentals of the anatomy of the human brain.

THE HUMAN BRAIN

So then let's have a quick look at the human brain. Even if you feel like yours is substantially underutilized compared to its capacity, it is still a marvel of incredible capability.

The following section is somewhat academic. Much like the law of gravity, you need not know all the detail to accept that the law is true. You will experience for yourself that you none the less subject to laws of gravity. However, having a working understanding of what is going helps you make sense of your experience in this world. In the same way, you need not know all the details about the anatomy of your brain, however developing a working understanding will help you make sense of your experience in your own body.

More importantly it will support you as you begin to make choices between instinctive reactions and select intentional responses to change your personal experiences.

The nervous system, which alongside the peripheral nervous system is responsible for regulating all bodily functions, is made up of the spinal cord, then the brain stem and above that the brain. The brain is made up of several of organs built in three primary layers each just above the other one: the hindbrain, the midbrain and the forebrain.

THE HINDBRAIN

The hindbrain is the well-protected central core of the brain. It includes the cerebellum, reticular formation and brain stem. They are responsible for some of the most basic autonomic functions of life, such as breathing and movement.

The brain stem contains the pons and medulla oblongata. Evolutionarily speaking, the hindbrain contains the oldest parts of the brain, which all vertebrates possess, though they may look different from species to species.

THE MIDBRAIN

The midbrain makes up part of the brain stem. It is located between the hindbrain and forebrain.

All sensory and motor information that travels between the forebrain and the spinal cord passes through the midbrain, making it a relay station for the central nervous system.

THE FOREBRAIN

The forebrain is the most anterior division of the developing vertebrate brain, containing the most complex networks in the central nervous system. The lower division contains the thalamus and hypothalamus (which together form the limbic system). The upper contains the cerebrum, the home of the highest-level cognitive processing in the brain.

It is the large and complicated forebrain that distinguishes the human brain from other vertebrate brains. The brain's lower-level structures consist of the brain stem and spinal cord, along with the cerebellum. These are the oldest parts of the brain, having existed for much of its evolutionary history. As such they are geared more toward basic bodily processes necessary to survival.

It is the more recent layers of the brain (the forebrain) which are responsible for the higher-level cognitive functioning (language, reasoning) which are not strictly necessary to keep a body alive.

The hindbrain, which includes the medulla oblongata, the pons, and the cerebellum, is responsible some of the oldest and most primitive body functions.

THE MEDULLA OBLONGATA

The medulla oblongata sits at the transition zone between the brain and the spinal cord. It is the first region that formally belongs to the brain (rather than the spinal cord). It is the control center for respiratory, cardiovascular, and digestive functions.

The pons connects the medulla oblongata with the midbrain region and also relays signals from the forebrain to the cerebellum. It houses the control centers for respiration and inhibitory functions. The cerebellum is attached to the dorsal side of the pons.

THE CEREBELLUM

The cerebellum is a separate region of the brain behind the medulla oblongata and pons. It is attached to the rest of the brain by three stalks and coordinates skeletal muscles to produce smooth, graceful motions.

The cerebellum receives information from our eyes, ears, muscles, and joints about the body's current positioning referred to as the process of proprioception. It also receives output from the cerebral cortex about where these body parts should be.

After processing this information, the cerebellum sends motor impulses from the brain stem to the skeletal muscles so they can move. The main function of the cerebellum is this muscle coordination. It is also responsible for balance and posture, and it assists us when we are learning a new motor skill, such as playing a sport or musical instrument.

> [Activation code] The cerebellum receives information from our eyes, ears, muscles and joints about the body's current positioning referred to as the process of proprioception.

THE MIDBRAIN

The midbrain is located between the hindbrain and forebrain, but it is actually part of the brain stem. It displays the same basic functional composition found in the spinal cord and the hindbrain.

Ventral areas control motor function and convey motor information from the cerebral cortex. Dorsal regions of the midbrain are involved in sensory information circuits. The substantia nigra, a part of the midbrain that plays a role in reward, addiction and movement due to its high levels of dopaminergic neurons.

THE INTERBRAIN

The diencephalon (or interbrain) is the region of the embryonic vertebrate neural tube that gives rise to posterior forebrain structures. In adults, the diencephalon appears at the upper end of the brain stem, between the cerebrum and the brain stem. It is home to the limbic system, which is considered to be the seat of emotion in the human brain.

THE THALAMUS

The thalamus is part of the limbic system. It comprises two lobes of grey matter along the bottom of the cerebral cortex.

Because nearly all sensory information passes through the thalamus it is considered the sensory "way station" of the brain, passing information on to the cerebral cortex (which is in the forebrain).

Lesions of, or stimulation to, the thalamus are associated with changes in emotional reactivity.

However, the importance of this structure on the regulation of emotion-related responses is not due to the activity of the thalamus itself, but to the connections between the thalamus and other limbic-system structures.

THE HYPOTHALAMUS

The hypothalamus is a small part of the brain located just below the thalamus. Lesions of the hypothalamus interfere with motivated behaviors like sexuality, combativeness, and hunger.

The hypothalamus also plays a role in emotion: parts of the hypothalamus seem to be involved in pleasure and rage, while the central part is linked to aversion, displeasure, and a tendency towards uncontrollable and loud laughing. When external stimuli are presented (for example, a dangerous stimulus), the hypothalamus sends signals to other limbic areas to trigger feeling states in response to the stimuli (in this case, fear).

THE NERVOUS SYSTEM

THE SPINAL CORD

The spinal cord is a tail-like structure embedded in the vertebral canal of the spine. The adult spinal cord is about 40cm long and weighs approximately 30g.

The spinal cord is attached to the underside of the medulla oblongata and is organized to serve four distinct tasks; to convey mainly sensory information to the brain, to carry information generated in the brain to peripheral targets like skeletal muscles, to control nearby organs via the autonomic nervous system and to enable sensorimotor functions to control posture and other fundamental movements.

THE CEREBRAL CORTEX

The cerebral cortex, the largest part of the mammalian brain, is the wrinkly gray outer covering of the cerebrum. While the cortex is about half a centimeter thick, it is here that all sensation, perception, memory, association, thought, and voluntary physical actions take place. The cerebral cortex is considered the ultimate control and information-processing centre in the brain.

The cortex is made of layers of neurons with many inputs. These cortical neurons function like mini microprocessors or logic gates. It contains glial cells, which guide neural connections, provides nutrients and myelin to neurons, and absorb extra ions and neurotransmitters. The cortex is divided into four different lobes (the parietal, occipital, temporal, and frontal lobes) each with a different specific function.

THE CEREBRUM

Beneath the cerebral cortex is the cerebrum, which serves as the main thought and control center of the brain.

> [Activation code] It is the seat of higher-level thought like emotions and decision making (as opposed to lower-level thought like balance, movement, and reflexes).

The cerebrum is composed of gray and white matter. Gray matter is the mass of all the cell bodies, dendrites, and synapses of neurons interlaced with one another, while white matter consists of the long, myelin-coated axons of those neurons connecting masses of gray matter to each other.

BRAIN HEMISPHERES

The brain is divided into two halves, called hemispheres. The two hemispheres communicate with one another through the corpus callosum. There is evidence that each brain hemisphere has its own distinct functions, a phenomenon referred to as lateralization.

The left hemisphere appears to dominate the functions of speech, language processing and comprehension, and logical reasoning, while the right is more dominant in spatial tasks like vision-independent object recognition (such as identifying an object by touch or another non-visual senses).

The differences between the functions of the left and right hemispheres can be easily exaggerated. Both hemispheres are involved with most processes. We are learning that neuroplasticity which is the ability of a brain to adapt to experience also enables the brain to compensate for damage to one hemisphere by taking on extra functions in the other half, especially in young brains. Further to the hemispheres, the brain is separated into four lobes; viz; the frontal, temporal, occipital, and parietal lobes.

THE FRONTAL LOBE

The frontal lobe is associated with executive functions and motor performance. Executive functions are some of the highest-order cognitive processes that humans have.

[Activation code] Examples of executive functions include planning and engaging in goal-directed behaviour, been able to recognize future consequences of one's current actions, the ability to choose between good and bad actions, developing a working understanding of socially acceptable responses and determining similarities & differences between objects or situations.

The frontal lobe is considered to be the moral center of the brain because it is responsible for advanced decision-making processes. It also plays an important role in retaining emotional memories derived from the limbic system and modifying those emotions to fit socially accepted norms.

THE TEMPORAL LOBE

The temporal lobe is associated with the retention of short and long-term memories. It processes sensory input including auditory information, language comprehension, and naming.

It also creates emotional responses and controls biological drives such as aggression and sexuality. The temporal lobe contains the hippocampus which is the memory center of the brain. The hippocampus plays a key role in the formation of emotion-laden, long-term memories based on emotional input from the amygdala.

THE OCCIPITAL LOBE

The occipital lobe contains most of the visual cortex and is the visual processing center of the brain. Cells on the posterior side of the occipital lobe are arranged as a spatial map of the retinal field.

The visual cortex receives raw sensory information through sensors in the retina of the eyes, which is then conveyed through the optic tracts to the visual cortex.

THE PARIETAL LOBE

The parietal lobe is associated with sensory skills. It integrates different types of sensory information and is particularly useful in spatial processing and navigation.

The parietal lobe plays an important role in integrating sensory information from various parts of the body, understanding numbers and their relations, and manipulating objects. It also processes information related to the sense of touch.

THE LIMBIC SYSTEM

The limbic system combines higher mental functions and primitive emotion into one system. It is a complex set of structures found on the central underside of the cerebrum, comprising inner sections of the temporal lobes and the bottom of the frontal lobe. It is often referred to as the emotional nervous system.

Emotional life is largely housed in the limbic system. It is not only responsible for our emotional lives but also our higher mental functions like learning and formation of memories. The limbic system is the reason that some physical experiences like eating seem so pleasurable and the reason why some medical conditions, such as high blood pressure, are caused by mental stress. There are several important structures within the limbic system: the amygdala, hippocampus, thalamus, hypothalamus, basal ganglia, and cingulate gyrus.

The limbic system operates by influencing the endocrine system and the autonomic nervous system. It is highly interconnected with the nucleus accumbens, which plays a role in sexual arousal and the "high" derived from certain recreational drugs. These responses are heavily modulated by dopaminergic projections from the limbic system.

> [Activation code] Your emotional life is largely housed in the limbic system, responsible for both our emotional lives and higher mental functions like learning and formation of memories.

THE AMYGDALA

The amygdala is a small almond-shaped structure; there is one located in each of the left and right temporal lobes. Also known as the emotional center of the brain, the amygdala is involved in evaluating the emotional valence of situations (e.g., happy, sad, scary). It helps the brain recognize potential threats and helps prepare the body for fight-or-flight reactions by increasing heart and breathing rate.

The amygdala is also responsible for learning on the basis of reward or punishment. Due to its close proximity to the hippocampus, the amygdala is involved in the modulation of memory consolidation, particularly emotionally-laden memories. Emotional arousal following a learning event influences the strength of the subsequent memory of that event, so that greater emotional arousal following a learning event enhances a person's retention of that memory.

[Activation code] The amygdala is also responsible for learning on the basis of reward or punishment. The greater the emotional arousal following a learning event the more enhanced is a person's retention of that memory.

THE HIPPOCAMPUS

The hippocampus is found deep in the temporal lobe and is shaped like a seahorse. It consists of two horns curving back from the amygdala. Psychologists and neuroscientists dispute the precise role of the hippocampus, but generally agree that it plays an essential role in the formation of new memories about past experiences.

Some researchers consider the hippocampus to be responsible for general declarative memory (memories that can be explicitly verbalized, such as the memory of facts and episodic memory). Both the thalamus and hypothalamus are associated with changes in emotional reactivity. The thalamus, which is a sensory "way-station" for the rest of the brain, is important because of its connections with other limbic-system structures.

THE HYPOTHALAMUS

The hypothalamus is a small part of the brain located just below the thalamus on both sides of the third ventricle. Lesions of the hypothalamus interfere with several unconscious functions (such as respiration and metabolism) and some 'motivated' behaviors like sexuality, combativeness, and hunger.

The lateral parts of the hypothalamus seem to be involved with pleasure and rage, while the medial part is linked to aversion, displeasure, and a tendency for uncontrollable and loud laughter. The cingulate gyrus is located in the medial side of the brain next to the corpus callosum.

There is still much to be learned about this gyrus, but it is known that its frontal part links smells and sights with pleasant memories of previous emotions. This region also participates in our emotional reaction to pain and in the regulation of aggressive behavior.

THE BASAL GANGLIA

The basal ganglia is a group of nuclei lying deep in the subcortical white matter of the frontal lobes that organizes motor behavior. The caudate, putamen and globus pallidus are major components of the basal ganglia.

The basal ganglia appear to serve as a gating mechanism for physical movements, inhibiting potential movements until they are fully appropriate for the circumstances in which they are to be executed.

The basal ganglia is also involved with rule-based habit learning (e.g., initiating, stopping, monitoring, temporal sequencing, and maintaining the appropriate movement). It participates in inhibiting undesired movements and permitting desired ones as well as our ability to choosing from potential actions. As well as motor planning, sequencing, predictive control along with working memory and attention.

NEUROPLASTICITY

The brain is constantly adapting throughout a lifetime, though sometimes over critical, genetically determined periods of time. Neuroplasticity is the brain's ability to create new neural pathways to account for learning based on the acquisition of new experiences.

It refers to changes in neural pathways and synapses that result from changes in behavior, environmental and neural processes. It can also result from changes as a consequence of bodily injury. What I want you to hear me say is that Neuroplasticity has replaced the formerly held theory that the brain is a physiologically static organ and explores how the brain changes throughout life.

Neuroplasticity occurs on a variety of levels, ranging from minute cellular changes resulting from learning to large-scale cortical remapping in response to injury. The role of neuroplasticity is widely recognized in healthy development, learning, memory, and recovery from brain damage.

During most of the 20th century, the consensus among neuroscientists was that brain structure is relatively immutable after a critical period during early childhood. It is true that the brain is especially "plastic" during childhood's critical period with new neural connections forming constantly.

> [Activation code] Neuroplasticity has replaced the formerly held theory that the brain is a physiologically static organ.

More recent findings, however, show that many aspects of the brain remain plastic even into adulthood. Plasticity can be demonstrated over the course of virtually any form of learning. For one to remember an experience, the circuitry of the brain must change. Learning takes place when there is either a change in the internal structure of neurons or a heightened number of synapses between neurons.

A surprising consequence of neuroplasticity is that the brain activity associated with a given function can move to a different location; this can result from normal experience and also occurs in the process of recovery from brain injury. To point to this fact neuroplasticity is the basis of goal-directed experiential therapeutic programs in rehabilitation after brain injury.

Take for example a person who is blinded in one eye. The part of the brain associated with processing input from that eye doesn't simply sit idle. Over time it takes on new functions, perhaps processing visual input from the remaining eye or doing something else entirely. This is because while certain parts of the brain have a typical function, the brain can be "rewired", all because of (neuro) plasticity.

UNPACKING THE INSIGHTS

There is something that I really want you to see. If you were here in the room with as I write this you would see just how excited I get working on this manuscript. I really want people to get this. When you see what I have seen I am convinced that you will have a set of insights that can change your life forever, or your experience as you journey through this life at least. To prepare you for this I want you to understand three simple concepts that will make for the learning you are about to embrace.

COGNITION

First is the concept of cognition, the mental action or process of gaining knowledge and understanding through thought, experience, and the senses.

Human cognition is simultaneously conscious and unconscious, concrete or abstract, as well as intuitive (like knowledge of a language) and conceptual (like a model of a language). Cognitive processes use existing knowledge and generate new knowledge.

ALERTNESS

Next is the concept of alertness. This is the state of active attention by high sensory awareness such as being watchful and prompt to meet danger or emergency or being quick to perceive and act. It is related to psychology as well as to physiology.

AWARENESS

The third concept I want you to be mindful of is the notion of Awareness. This is the ability to directly know and perceive, to feel, to be conscious or be in the state of having knowledge of events.

LESSONS FROM HUMAN VISION

There is a significant lesson to be learned from the human visual system which gives our bodies the ability to see the physical environment in which we live. The system requires communication between its major sensory organ (the eye) and the core of the central nervous system (the brain) to interpret external stimuli (light waves) as images. Developing a functional understanding of this process will help you understand the physiology of your emotion-related behavioral responses.

VISUAL PERCEPTION

All vision is based on the perception of electromagnetic rays. These rays pass through the cornea in the form of light; the cornea focuses the rays as they enter the eye through the pupil, the black aperture at the front of the eye. The pupil acts as a gatekeeper, allowing as much or as little light to enter as is necessary to see an image properly.

VISUAL RECEPTION

Behind the pupil is the lens, which is similar in shape and function to a camera lens. Together with the cornea, the lens adjusts the focal length of the image being seen onto the back of the eye, the retina. Visual reception occurs at the retina where photoreceptor cells called cones and rods give an image color and shadow.

AN IMAGE TRANSDUCED

The image of the object perceived by the eye is transduced into neural impulses and then transferred through the optic nerve to the rest of the brain for processing. The visual cortex in the brain interprets the image to extract form, meaning, memory, and context.

Color vision is a critical component of human vision and plays an important role in both perception and communication. Color sensors are found within cones, which respond to relatively broad color bands in the three basic regions of red, green, and blue (RGB). Any colors in between these three are perceived as different linear combinations of RGB.

[Activation code] The visual cortex in the brain interprets the image to extract form, *meaning, memory, and *context.

CHEMICAL AND ELECTRICAL SIGNALS

The eye is much more sensitive to overall light and color intensity than changes in the color itself. Colors have three attributes: brightness, based on luminance and reflectivity; saturation, based on the amount of white present; and hue, based on color combinations.

Sophisticated combinations of these receptors signals are transduced into chemical and electrical signals, which are sent to the brain for the dynamic process of color perception.

A SET OF PROCESSES

Perception refers to the set of processes we use to make sense of all the stimuli you encounter every second, from the glow of the computer screen in front of you to the smell of the room to the sudden itch that feels like an insect bite on your ankle.

Our perceptions are based on how we interpret all these different sensations, which are sensory impressions we get from the stimuli in the world around us. Perception enables us to navigate the world and to make decisions about everything, from which of our favorite T-shirt's to wear or how fast to run away from danger.

[Activation code] Perception refers to the set of processes we use to make sense of all the stimuli you encounter every second.

Would you like to experience this for yourself?

Before you do anything further, when I say so, I want you to close your eyes for a count of five. Listen, don't cheat now, alright! Before you close your eyes read the following three sentences without looking around.

- What do you remember about the room you are in?
- What is the color of the walls, the angle of the shadows?
- Ready, now go ahead and with your eyes closed think about those three things.

SELECTIVE ATTENTION

Whether or not we know it, we selectively attend to different things in our environment. Our brains simply don't have the capacity to attend to every single detail in the world around us.

The perceptual process is a sequence of steps that begins with stimuli in the environment and ends with our interpretation of those stimuli. This process is typically unconscious and happens hundreds of thousands of times a day.

AN UNCONSCIOUS PROCESS

An unconscious process is one that happens without awareness or intention. When you open your eyes, you do not need to tell your brain to interpret the light falling onto your retinas from the object in front of you as "computer" because this has happened unconsciously.

When you step out into a chilly night, your brain does not need to be told "cold" because the stimuli trigger the processes and categories automatically.

SELECTION DECISION

The world around us is filled with an infinite number of stimuli that we might attend to, but our brains do not have the resources to pay attention to everything. So the first step of perception is the (usually unconscious, but sometimes intentional) selection decision of what to attend to.

> [Activation code] The perceptual process begins with stimuli in the environment and ends with our interpretation of those stimuli.

ATTENDED STIMULUS

Depending on the environment, and depending on us as individuals, we might choose to focus on a familiar stimulus or something new. When we give attention to one specific thing in our environment, whether that is a smell, a feeling, a sound, or something else entirely, it becomes the attended stimulus.

NEURAL ORGANIZATION

Once we have chosen to attend to a stimulus in the environment, consciously or unconsciously although usually the latter, the choice sets off a series of reactions in our brain. This neural organization process starts with the activation of our sensory receptors; touch, taste, smell, sight, and hearing.

The receptors transduce the input energy into neural activity, which is transmitted to our brains, where we construct a mental representation of the stimulus (or, in most cases, the multiple related stimuli) called a percept.

INTERPRETATION

After we have dealt with a stimulus, and our brains have received and organized the information, we interpret it in a way that makes sense using our existing information about the world. Interpretation simply means that we take the information that we have sensed and organized and turn it into something that we can categorize.

CATEGORIZATION

For instance, in the well-known Rubin's Vase illusion some individuals will interpret the sensory information as "vase," while some will interpret it as "faces." The illusion is created by the pattern visible in the drawing. Depending on which shape is more familiar to you, you will identify with one shape over the other. This happens unconsciously thousands of times a day. By putting different stimuli into categories, we can better understand and react to the world around us.

This is how we develop 'consciousness', the state of awareness of the surrounding environment, our thoughts, and feelings or sensations. In order to experience consciousness, we must be both awake and aware.

CONSCIOUSNESS

Consciousness is the quality or state of being aware of an external object or something within oneself, such as thoughts, feelings, memories, or sensations. It has also been described as sentience, awareness, subjectivity, the ability to experience or to feel, wakefulness, having a sense of selfhood, and the executive-control system of the mind.

At one time, consciousness was viewed with skepticism by many scientists, but in recent years, it has become a significant topic of research in psychology and neuroscience. Despite the difficulty in coming to a definition, many philosophers believe that there is a broadly shared underlying intuition about what consciousness is.

Philosophers since the time of Descartes and Locke have struggled to comprehend the nature of consciousness and pin down its essential properties. Issues of concern in the philosophy of consciousness include the following: whether consciousness can ever be explained mechanistically; whether non-human consciousness exists, and if so, how it can be recognized; how consciousness relates to language; whether consciousness can be understood in a way that does not require a dualistic distinction between mental and physical states or properties; and whether it may ever be possible for computers or robots to be conscious.

[Activation code] In order to develop consciousness...you must be both awake and aware.

THE MIND-BODY PROBLEM

The mind-body problem is essentially the problem of consciousness. It is the journey to understand how mental experiences arise from a physical entity. How are our mental states, beliefs, actions, and thinking related to our physical states, bodily functions, and external events, given that the body is physical and the mind is non-physical?

THE REALM OF THOUGHT

The first and most important philosopher to address this conundrum was René Descartes in the 17th century, and his answer was termed Cartesian dualism. The explanation behind Cartesian dualism is that consciousness resides within an immaterial domain he called 'res cogitans' (the realm of thought), rather than in the domain of material things, which he called 'res extensa' (the realm of extension).

He suggested that the interaction between these two domains occurs inside the brain. He further suggested the pineal gland as the point of interaction, but was later challenged several times on this claim. These challenges sparked some key initial research on consciousness.

For over 2000 years questions surrounding human consciousness, such as how the everyday inner workings of our brains give rise to a single cohesive reality and a sense of an individual self, have been baffling philosophers from Plato to Descartes. Descartes, as previously mentioned, is noted for his dualist theory of consciousness, in which the physical body is separate from the immaterial mind. He also gave us the most famous summary of human consciousness: "I think, therefore I am."

> [Activation code] He suggested that the interaction between these two domains occurs inside the brain.

CONSCIOUSNESS ENGENDERED

The historical materialism of Karl Marx rejects the mind-body dichotomy and holds that consciousness is engendered by the material contingencies of one's environment. John Locke, another early philosopher, claimed that consciousness, and therefore personal identity, are independent of all substances.

He pointed out that there is no reason to assume that consciousness is tied to any particular body or mind, or that consciousness cannot be transferred from one body or mind to another.

American psychologist William James compared consciousness to a stream, unbroken and continuous despite constant shifts and changes. While the focus of much of the research in psychology shifted to purely observable behaviors during the first half of the twentieth century, research on human consciousness has grown tremendously since the 1950s.

BIOLOGICAL AND PSYCHOLOGICAL

Today, the primary focus of consciousness research is on understanding what consciousness means both biologically and psychologically. It questions what it means for information to be present in consciousness, and seeks to determine the neural and psychological correlates of consciousness.

Issues of interest include phenomena such as perception, subliminal perception, blindsight, anosognosia, brainwaves during sleep, and altered states of consciousness produced by psychoactive drugs or spiritual or meditative techniques.

The majority of experimental studies assess consciousness by asking human subjects for a verbal report of their experiences. However, in order to confirm the significance of these verbal reports, scientists must compare them to the activity that simultaneously takes place in the brain, that is, they must look for the neural correlates of consciousness.

CONSCIOUSNESS AND EXECUTIVE FUNCTIONS

Higher brain areas are more widely accepted as necessary for consciousness to occur, especially the prefrontal cortex, which is involved in a range of higher cognitive functions collectively known as executive functions.

UNPACKING YOUR CHEMISTRY

Now that you have a foundational yet pragmatic understanding of the primary organs and components that make up your brain I hope that you will have a more thorough perspective and develop a better understanding of how you work.

More importantly that you get a working understanding of what is actually going on when you react to stimuli in the context of the environment that you find yourself in. The next layer of understanding I want to introduce to you is that of the chemicals and hormones that are at play in any given physiological process as you make sense of each stimulus.

This is where I want to describe each of these in so much as to create a basic working understanding of their function and role.

CREATING AROUSAL

Arousal is a state of alertness and activation. When aroused the person pays attention to certain things and is ready for action. We can become aroused in a number of ways. As arousal is linked to learning, decision and action, being able to arouse others is a useful skill.

NEUROTRANSMITTERS

Neurotransmitters are chemical messengers that enable neurotransmission across neurons. Neurons form elaborate networks through which nerve impulses travel. Each neuron has thousands of connections with neighboring neurons.

Neurons do not touch each other (except in the case of an electrical synapse through a gap junction); instead, neurons interact at contact points called synapses: a junction within two nerve cells, consisting of a miniature gap within which impulses are carried by a neurotransmitter. A neuron transports its information by way of a nerve impulse from a neuron on one nerve cell to another "target" neuron, muscle cell, or gland cell.

DOPAMINE

The well-known neurotransmitter called Dopamine has a number of important functions in the brain; including regulation of motor behavior, pleasures related to motivation and also emotional arousal. Because dopamine is the chemical that promotes feelings of pleasure, it makes us look forward to seek pleasure and enjoy life and various activities.

Sometimes called "The Molecule of Happiness," dopamine tends to be the scientific explanation for why we can be happy or experience satisfaction. In the prefrontal cortex, the main part of the brain associated with higher-ordered thinking, dopamine secretions help to improve your working memory.

[Activation code] The neurotransmitter Dopamine promotes feelings of pleasure and helps to improve your working memory. It is often called the molecule of happiness.

SEROTONIN

Serotonin is a monoamine neurotransmitter considered the pleasure and mood hormone. It is mostly produced by and found in the intestine (approximately 90%), and the remainder in central nervous system neurons.

It functions to regulate appetite, sleep, memory and learning, temperature, mood, behaviour, muscle contraction, and function of the cardiovascular system, endocrine system and the endorphins that increase our sense of well-being and improve our humor.

[Activation code] The neurotransmitter Serotonin, mostly produced in the gut, is sometimes called the happy hormone as it increases our sense of wellbeing.

ADRENALINE

Adrenaline (or epinephrine) and noradrenline are two separate but related hormones and neurotransmitters. They are released into the bloodstream and serve as chemical mediators, and also convey the nerve impulses to various organs.

Adrenaline has many different actions depending on the type of cells it is acting upon. The overall effect of adrenaline is to prepare the body for the 'fight or flight' response in response to a stimuli of stress. It plays an important role in the fight-or-flight response by increasing blood flow to muscles, output of the heart, pupil dilation, and blood sugar.

[Activation code] The primary role of adrenaline is to prepare the body for the 'fight-or-fight' response.

NORADRENALIN

Norepinephrine (noradrenaline) (NE), also called noradrenaline (NA) or noradrenalin. The general function of norepinephrine is to mobilize the brain and body for action.

Norepinephrine release is highest during wakefulness, and reaches much higher levels during situations of stress or danger, in the so-called fight-or-flight response.

In the brain, norepinephrine increases arousal and alertness, promotes vigilance, enhances the formation and retrieval of memory, and focuses attention; it also increases restlessness and anxiety. Norepinephrine is the main neurotransmitter used by the sympathetic nervous system.

STRESS

We see Stress to mean any situation that threatens the continued stability of the body and its functions. Stress affects a wide variety of body systems: the two most consistently activated are the hypothalamic-pituitary-adrenal axis and the norepinephrine system.

This includes both the sympathetic nervous system and the locus coeruleus-centered system, part of the ascending reticular activating system (ARAS) in the brain. Stressors of many types evoke increases in noradrenergic activity, which mobilizes the brain and body to meet the threat.

CORTISOL

Cortisol is produced from cholesterol in the two adrenal glands located on top of each kidney. It is normally released in response to events and circumstances such as waking up in the morning, exercising, and acute stress. Cortisol's far-reaching, systemic effects play many roles in the body's effort to carry out its processes and maintain homeostasis.

Cortisol (along with its partner epinephrine) is best known for its involvement in the "fight-or-flight" response and temporary increase in energy production, at the expense of processes that are not required for immediate survival. The stress response operates as intended as the mechanism for survival.

First, you will face (i) a stressor, something that causes a state of strain or tension. Your body then responds with the sudden release of (ii) hormones, a large number in rapid succession while the adrenals secrete (iii) cortisol.

Cortisol prepares the body for a fight-or-flight response by flooding it with glucose, supplying an immediate energy source to large muscles. This cortisol (iv) inhibits insulin production in an attempt to prevent glucose from being stored, favoring its immediate use.

Cortisol also (v) narrows the arteries while the epinephrine increases heart rate, both of which force blood to pump harder and faster. You then address the situation and (vi) seek a resolution. The (vii) hormone levels then return to normal.

[Activation code] Cortisol is best known for its involvement in the 'fight-or-flight' response and temporary increase in energy production, at the expense of processes that are not required for immediate survival.

THE RETICULAR ACTIVATING SYSTEM

This system is considered the brain's attention center and the seat of motivation. The ascending reticular activating system (often referred to as the RAS) is connected to the spinal cord at its base from where it accepts information which comes from the ascending sensory tracts directly.

It travels up to the midbrain and while going up forms a complex neuron collection that acts as a convergence point for signals from both the interior environment as well as your external surroundings.

So, the RAS is a place where your thoughts, internal feelings and the outside influences converge. It is very skilled in producing dynamic effects on the motor activity centers located in the brain and the cortex activity such as the frontal lobes.

The most important function of RAS is to regulate the shift between sleep and wakefulness. The transition made by our body from a deep slumber to being completely awake as well as functional and vice versa is under the control of this system. It also plays a vital role during our sleep and when we 'see' dreams.

It is also responsible for supplying an integrated response to outside stimuli. The skill to act as a filter of information brought out by the external sources and to pinpoint a particular fact with detailed thought is the controlled effect of the reticular activating system. Coordination while walking, eating or sexual functions are carried out by the RAS.

A simple way of describing the function of the RAS is a bundle of nerves at our brainstem that filters out unnecessary information so that only the most relevant and important stuff gets through.

Your RAS takes what you focus on and creates a filter for it. It then sifts through the data and presents only the pieces that are important to you. All of this happens without you noticing, of course. The RAS programs itself to work in your favor without you actively doing anything.

It is important to note that in a similar way, the RAS seeks information that validates your beliefs. It filters the world through the parameters you give it, and your beliefs shape those parameters. If you think you are bad at giving speeches, you probably will be. If you believe you work efficiently, you most likely do. The RAS helps you see what you want to see and in doing so, influences your actions.

The ascending reticular activating system (ARAS), also known simply as the reticular activating system (RAS), is a set of connected nuclei in the brains of vertebrates responsible for regulating wakefulness and sleep-wake transitions.

[Activation code] The RAS will automatically seek out and indentify information which will validate your beliefs.

OPERANT CONDITIONING

Understanding the function and role of the RAS will help you appreciate operant conditioning. A behavior will increase if it is followed by positive reinforcement. It will decrease if it is followed by punishment. Operant Conditioning can be described as 'learning by consequences'.

[Activation code] A particular behavior will increase if that (desired) behavior it is followed by (intentional) positive reinforcement.

Classical conditioning involves automatic, pre-programmed responses, whereas operant conditioning involves learned behaviors. Classical conditioning is more about the push of stimulus while operant conditioning is more about the pull of reward or other consequences.

Making sense of this pull that will help you understand why you display the behavior response the way that you do, especially when you don't really want to. It will also help you to develop a functional understanding of some of the primary drivers that influence human behavior.

MASLOW'S HIERARCHY OF NEEDS

In 1943 Abraham Maslow, one of the founding fathers of humanist approaches to management, wrote an influential paper that set out five fundamental human needs. A key aspect of the model is the hierarchical nature of the needs.

THE FIVE FUNDAMENTAL HUMAN NEEDS

Self-actualization needs

At the top of the initial model on the fifth level, we find Self-actualization. Thus is the need to 'become what we are capable of becoming', which would be our greatest achievement.

Esteem needs

On the fourth level are the esteem needs. This has to do with the desire and aspiration for a higher position within a group. If people respect us, we enjoy a sense of having greater power.

Belonging needs

The third level are the belonging needs which introduce our tribal nature. If we are helpful and kind to others they will want us as friends as part of a community or tribe.

Safety needs

The next level are the safety needs which are about putting a roof over our heads and keeping us from harm. If we are rich, strong and powerful, or have good friends, we can make ourselves safe.

Physiological needs

Depicted on the lowest or first level Maslow introduced Physiological needs which have to do with the maintenance of the human body. If we are unwell, then little else matters until we recover.

Maslow later added three more needs by splitting two of the above five needs. Between esteem and self-actualization two needs were added;

Know and understand

The need to know and understand explains the cognitive need of the academic.

Aesthetic beauty

The need for aesthetic beauty is the emotional need of the artist.

Self-actualization was divided into:

Self-actualization, which is realizing one's own potential, as above.

and Transcendence

Transcendence, which is helping others to achieve their potential and enjoy a sense of greater service.

MUMFORD'S NEEDS

Another important contribution to the body of knowledge understanding human behavior was made by Mumford (1976) who observed that employees did not simply see their job as a means to an end, and had needs which related to the nature of their work.

Knowledge needs

Individuals desire work that adequately utilizes their knowledge and skills.

To do a job, employees need several kinds of knowledge, including 'professional' knowledge about the discipline, 'procedural' knowledge on how to do a particular job, 'locational' knowledge on what can be found where and 'social' knowledge on how to influence others.

Psychological needs

As with all people, employees have inner human needs such as recognition, responsibility, status and advancement.

A problem can occur where employers treat their people as machines to be commanded and ignore their psychological needs.

Task needs

We have needs around what we do, including having meaningful work and some degree of autonomy to be able to achieve success under our own steam.

Moral needs

Related to psychological needs, we have the need to be treated as intelligent and valued people. In other words, employers should treat employees in the way they would themselves wish to be treated.

Part two

GETTING YOUR POWER BACK

What happened to my power?
STRATEGIES FOR SELF REGULATION

EMOTIONAL INTELLIGENCE

Emotional Intelligence (EQ) is a neat metaphor that borrows from the notion of IQ. It implies that some people are better at handling emotions than others. It also hints that you might be able to increase your EQ. Practically it offers a useful set of guidelines for doing just this.

Being emotionally self-aware means knowing how you feel in "real time." Self-knowledge is the first step in being able to handle emotions. If you can see them and name them, then you at least have a chance to do something about them.

EMPATHY

Empathy is the ability to feel and understand the emotions of others. If you can empathize, you can bring about a sense of trust, as people desperately want to be understood at the emotional level.

All great caregivers and nurturers major in empathy and compassion. The ability to balance emotion and reason in making decisions leads to good or better quality decisions. I am not suggesting that emotion should be abandoned, it prevents us from making less cold and callous decisions. In a similar way logic should not be abandoned unless you can be content with a wishy-washy outcome.

> [Activation code] Empathy is the ability to feel and understand the emotions of others.

Emotional Intelligence means developing cognitive awareness to take primary responsibility for your own emotions and happiness. You cannot say that others "made" you feel the way you feel.

> [Activation code] Emotional Intelligence means developing the cognitive awareness to take primary responsibility for your own emotions and happiness.

REGULATION OF EMOTION

Self-regulation of emotion is the ability to respond to the ongoing demands of experience with the range of emotions in a manner that is socially tolerable and sufficiently flexible to permit spontaneous reactions. It also develops your ability to delay spontaneous reactions as you need to. It can also be defined as extrinsic and intrinsic processes responsible for monitoring, evaluating, and modifying emotional reactions.

Emotional regulation is a complex process that involves initiating (to begin), inhibiting (to prohibit or prevent), or modulating (to control) your state or chosen behavioral response in a given situation. This includes your subjective experience (feelings), cognitive responses (thoughts), emotion-related physiological responses (for example heart rate or hormonal activity), and emotion-related behavior (bodily actions or expressions).

Emotional regulation can also be used to describe processes such as the tendency to focus your attention to a task and the ability to manage your emotional response so as to suppress inappropriate behavior under intrinsic instruction. For this reason I trust you will agree that emotional regulation is a highly significant function to master in human life.

THE EXPERIENCE OF EMOTION IN THE BODY

I am often asked to help create a better understanding of the experience of emotion in the human body. More often than not this is a request from a left brain or typically concrete and analytical thinker.

Nummenmaa et al. (2012) produced an innovative 'heat map', showing where emotions are experienced and the intensity of the feeling. This was done by offering subjects (from both Europe and Asia) emotional words, stories, movies and facial expressions. They were then asked to identify the emotion and describe the bodily sensations they experienced associated with each.

EXPERIENCING EMOTIONS IN THE BODY

In the examples below they are described by the emotion experienced and its location and intensity:

Anger; Fairly evenly across upper torso, head and arms. Hottest in heart, hands, face. A little sensation in lower legs.

Fear; Warm across upper torso with some in the lower torso. A little in arms and less in the legs. Some in head, but not in the lower face.

Disgust; Lightly warm upper body, head and hands. Hottest in lower face and the lower abdomen.

Happiness; Warm all over the body. Hottest in heart and head and some down the arms.

Sadness; Cold arms and legs, especially lower legs. A little heat in heart, neck and eyes.

Surprise; Slightly cool legs. Warm chest and head. Warmest around eyes.

Neutral; Just a little coolness around armpits.

Anxiety; Hot torso with hottest around the heart. Some warmth in the head. Some coolness in legs.

Love; Hot upper body, especially around heart, face and groin. Warm arms with a little warmth running down legs.

Depression; Cold legs and arms, with some coolness in the head and lower abdomen.

Contempt; Heat only in the upper central upper torso, hot only in the face. Some coolness around groin.

Pride; Hot upper body with most heat around the whole upper torso and face. Some warmth in the arms

Shame; Some warmth through the torso. Warm head and hot cheeks. Coolness in the arms and legs.

Envy; Some warmth in the upper torso. Greatest warmth in the head. A little coolness in the legs.

THE PROCESS MODEL

The process model of emotion regulation is based upon the modal model of emotion. The modal model of emotion suggests that the emotion generation process occurs in a particular sequence over time.

This sequence can be described as,

1. Situation; the sequence begins with a situation (real or imagined) that is emotionally relevant.
2. Attention; cognitive attention is then directed towards the emotional situation.
3. Appraisal; the emotional situation is evaluated and interpreted.
4. Response; an emotional response is generated, giving rise to loosely coordinated changes in experiential, behavioral, and physiological response systems.

Because an emotional response (4) can cause changes to a situation (1), this model involves a feedback loop from the response (4) to the situation (1). This feedback loop suggests that the emotion generation process can occur recursively, is ongoing, and remains dynamic.

CONTROL AND ADJUSTMENT

The process model suggests that each of these four points in the emotion generation process can be subjected to control and adjustment.

From this conceptualization, the process model proposes five different families of emotion regulation that correspond to the regulation of a particular point in the emotion generation process. They occur in the following order; i) Situation selection, ii) Situation modification, iii) Attention deployment, iv) Cognitive change and v) Response modulation.

CATEGORIES OF EMOTIONAL REGULATION

The process model also divides these emotion regulation strategies into two categories: antecedent-focused and response-focused. Antecedent-focused strategies (i.e., situation selection, situation modification, attention deployment, and cognitive change) occur before an emotional response is fully generated. Response-focused strategies (i.e., response modulation) occur after an emotional response is fully generated.

SITUATION SELECTION

Situation selection involves choosing to avoid or approach an emotionally relevant situation. If a person selects to avoid or disengage from an emotionally relevant situation, he or she is decreasing the likelihood of experiencing an emotion.

Alternatively, if a person selects to approach or engage with an emotionally relevant situation, he or she is increasing the likelihood of experiencing an emotion. Typical examples of situation selection may be seen interpersonally, such as when a parent removes his or her child from an emotionally unpleasant situation. Use of situation selection may also be seen in psychopathology. For example, avoidance of social situations to regulate emotions is particularly pronounced for those with social anxiety disorder and avoidant personality disorder.

Effective situation selection is not always an easy task. For instance, humans display difficulties predicting their emotional responses in future events. Therefore, they may have trouble making accurate and appropriate decisions about which emotionally relevant situations to approach or to avoid.

[Activation code] Situation selection involves choosing to avoid or approach an emotionally relevant situation.

SITUATION MODIFICATION

Situation modification involves efforts to modify a situation to change its emotional impact. Situation modification refers specifically to altering one's external, physical environment. Altering one's "internal" environment to regulate emotion is called cognitive change.

Examples of situation modification may include injecting humor into a speech to elicit laughter or extending the physical distance between oneself and another person.

[Activation code] Situation modification refers specifically to altering one's external, physical environment.

ATTENTIONAL (ATTENTION) DEPLOYMENT

Attention deployment involves directing one's attention towards or away from an emotional situation. Distraction, an example of attention deployment, is an early selection strategy, which involves diverting one's attention away from an emotional stimulus and towards other content.

DISTRACTION

Distraction has been shown to reduce the intensity of painful and emotional experiences, to decrease facial responding and neural activation in the amygdala associated with emotion, and as well as to ease emotional distress.

As opposed to reappraisal, individuals show a relative preference to engage in distraction when facing stimuli of high negative emotional intensity. We do this because distraction easily filters out high-intensity emotional content, which would otherwise be relatively difficult to appraise and process.

RUMINATION

Rumination, another example of attention deployment, is defined as the passive and repetitive focusing of one's attention on one's symptoms of distress and the causes and consequences of these symptoms.

Rumination is generally considered to be a maladaptive emotion regulation strategy as it tends to exacerbate emotional distress. It has also been implicated in a host of disorders including major depression.

WORRY

Worry, another example of attention deployment, involves directing one's attention to thoughts and images concerned with potentially negative events in the future. By focusing on these events, worrying serves to aid in the down-regulation of intense negative emotion and physiological activity.

While worry may sometimes involve problem-solving, incessant worry is generally considered maladaptive, being a common feature of anxiety disorder.

THOUGHT SUPPRESSION

Thought suppression, an example of attention deployment, involves efforts to redirect one's attention from specific thoughts and mental images to other content to modify one's emotional state.

Although thought suppression may provide temporary relief from undesirable thoughts, it may ironically end up spurring the production of even more unwanted thoughts. This strategy is generally considered maladaptive, being most associated with obsessive-compulsive disorder.

COGNITIVE CHANGE

Cognitive change involves changing how one appraises or assesses the value or quality of a situation so as to alter its emotional meaning.

REAPPRAISAL

Reappraisal, an example of cognitive change, is a late selection strategy, which involves reinterpreting the meaning of an event to alter its emotional impact. For example, this might involve reinterpreting an event by broadening one's perspective to see "the bigger picture." Reappraisal has been shown to effectively reduce physiological, subjective, and neural emotional responding. As opposed to distraction, individuals show a relative preference to engage in reappraisal when facing stimuli of low negative emotional intensity because these stimuli are relatively easy to appraise and process.

Reappraisal is generally considered to be an adaptive emotion-regulation strategy. Compared to suppression, which is correlated negatively with many psychological disorders, reappraisal can be associated with better interpersonal outcomes, and can be positively related to wellbeing. However, some researchers argue that context is important when evaluating the adaptability of a strategy, suggesting that in some contexts reappraisal may be maladaptive.

Get Activated

[Activation code] Cognitive change involves changing how you appraise the value or quality of a situation so as to alter its attached emotional meaning.

DISTANCING

Distancing, an example of cognitive change involves taking on an independent, third-person perspective when evaluating an emotional event. Distancing has been shown to be an adaptive form of self-reflection, facilitating the emotional processing of negative or harmful stimuli, reducing emotional and cardiovascular reactivity to negative stimuli, and increasing problem-solving behavior.

HUMOR

Humor, an example of cognitive change, has been shown to be an effective emotion regulation strategy. Specifically, positive, good-natured humor has been shown to effectively up-regulate positive emotion and down-regulate negative emotion. On the other hand, negative, mean-spirited humor is less effective in this regard.

RESPONSE MODULATION

Response modulation involves attempts to influence experiential, behavioral and physiological response systems.

EXPRESSIVE SUPPRESSION

Expressive suppression, an example of response modulation, involves inhibiting emotional expressions. It has been shown to reduce facial expressivity, subjective feelings of positive emotion, heart rate and sympathetic activation. However, the research is mixed regarding whether this strategy is effective for down-regulating negative emotion.

Research has also shown that expressive suppression may have negative social consequences, correlating with reduced personal connections and greater difficulties forming relationships. Expressive suppression is generally considered being a maladaptive emotion-regulation strategy.

Compared to reappraisal, it is correlated positively with many psychological disorders, associated with worse interpersonal outcomes, is negatively related to wellbeing, and requires the mobilization of a relatively substantial amount of cognitive resources. However, some researchers argue that context is important when evaluating the adaptability of a strategy, suggesting that in some contexts suppression may be adaptive.

DRUG USE

Drug use, an example of response modulation, can be a way to alter emotion-associated physiological responses. For example, alcohol can produce sedative and anxiolytic effects and beta blockers can affect sympathetic activation.

EXERCISE

Exercise, an example of response modulation, can be used to down-regulate the physiological and experiential effects of negative emotions. Regular physical activity has also been shown to reduce emotional distress and improve emotional control.

SLEEP

Sleep plays a role in emotion regulation although stress and worry can also interfere with sleep. Studies have shown that sleep, specifically REM sleep, down-regulates reactivity of the amygdala, a brain structure is known to be involved in the processing of emotions, in response to previous emotional experiences.

On the flip side, sleep deprivation is associated with greater emotional reactivity or overreaction to negative and stressful stimuli. This is a result of both increased amygdala activity and a disconnect between the amygdala and the prefrontal cortex, which regulates the amygdala through inhibition, together resulting in an overactive emotional brain.

Because of the subsequent lack of emotional control, we may associate sleep deprivation with depression, impulsivity, and mood swings. There is also evidence that sleep deprivation may reduce emotional reactivity to positive stimuli and impair emotion recognition in others.

THE ROLE OF EMOTION

As a professional speaker and master trainer, I am often asked to make an inspirational presentation as a 'motivational speaker'. My challenge is that I do not believe in the common understanding of the task that is I do not believe in the power of "motivation" or the magic of a "motivational" talk.

MOTIVES IN ACTION

I do however believe that this idea of motivation results from our "motives" put into action. The challenge is that very few people are willing to face up to their true motives. Even fewer are willing to do what it takes to take the necessary action. Let's unpack this concept a little further. I have heard it said that motivation, or motives in action, the 'e-motions' behind your values that drive particular action. They act to motivate you. Without emotion you would probably not do very much and hence would not survive, at least in the evolved form you are in now.

Motivations are felt in the body. Your muscles tense or relax. Your blood vessels dilate or contract. When you feel emotional, you also feel it physically. Therefore your emotions can make you feel uncomfortable or comfortable in your body, sending you signals to do something urgently or to stay in your comfortable state. Internal signals, for example, when you are trying to understand something or make a decision, you use your emotions to deduce whether what you have concluded is a good idea. Self-Perception Theory and the Cognitive Appraisal Theories of Emotion explain how you deduce your emotions by watching yourself.

YOUR EMOTION IS TALKING YOU TO YOU

When you think about something that contradicts your values, your emotions will tell you that it is bad. When you think about something that could hurt you, your emotions will tell you that this is not a good idea. Just by imagining what might happen, your emotions are still triggered and help you make better decisions.

EMOTIONAL SIGNALS

You generally wear your heart on your sleeve as your inner emotions are displayed on your outer body. Your face, in particular, has around 90 muscles, 30 of which have the sole purpose of signaling emotion to other people.

Social signals are very useful as they help others decide how to behave towards us. If someone is looking angry, then attacking them is probably not a good idea. If they are looking afraid then you could attack them or you could help them and thus earn their gratitude.

SELF CONCEPT

Self-concept is an understanding you have about yourself that are based on your personal experiences, body image, your thoughts, and how you tend to label yourself in various situations. A self-concept can also be defined as an all-encompassing awareness you had of yourself in the past; the awareness you have of yourself in the present, and the expectations you have of yourself at a future time.

Your self-concept is developed through a perception of yourself based on the knowledge you have gained over a lifetime of experience about your image, abilities, and in some ways a perception of your own individual uniqueness. This self perception is based on the information you have gathered about your values, life roles, goals, skills, and abilities over time.

Your self-concept is a collection of beliefs you have about your own nature, qualities, and behavior. It's about how you think and evaluate yourself at any given moment in time.

[Activation code] A self-concept is an understanding you have about yourself that are based on your personal experiences, body image, your thoughts, and how you tend to label yourself in various situations.

SELF IMAGE

Your self-image comes down to how you see yourself in the present moment. This includes the labels you give yourself about your personality and the beliefs you have about how the external world perceives you. It is important to note that your self-image isn't necessarily based on reality.

For instance, a person with anorexia may have a self-image that makes them believe they are obese, however in reality that is far from the truth. With this in mind, it is vitally important to recognize that a self-image is only your own perception of yourself and has no real basis in reality.

[Activation code] It is important to note that your self-image isn't necessarily based on reality.

SELF IDEAL

Your self-ideal is a percept of the person you wish you could be at any given moment in time, in the future-present-tense. This is your ideal self or the ideal person you envision of being and becoming.

More often than not the person we see ourselves as in the present tense, and the person that we want to become in the future-present tense do not match up. This is precisely what causes problems and often leads to self-sabotaging behavior patterns and is the cause of so much emotional struggle.

SELF ESTEEM

Your self-esteem encompasses your current emotional experiences. Moreover, it refers to the extent to which you like or approve of yourself or the extent to which you value yourself. You might have a positive or negative view of yourself. When you have a negative picture of yourself, you are seen as having low self-esteem.

This is often manifest in a lack of confidence and pessimism. On the other hand, when you have a favorable view of yourself you are seen as having high self-esteem. This is often manifest in a confident disposition, self-acceptance, and optimism.

ANXIETY

Anxiety is an emotion characterized by an unpleasant state of inner turmoil, often accompanied by the visible demonstration of nervous behavior like pacing back and forth, somatic complaints, and rumination. It is the subjectively unpleasant feelings of dread over anticipated events, such as the feeling of imminent death.

It is not the same as fear, which is a response to a real or a perceived immediate threat. Anxiety is the emotional distress associated with the expectation of a future threat.

COMING TO GRIPS WITH STRESS

Stress is the simple name for what happens when the body's emergency response is activated. A stressful event is one that activates your sympathetic (fight-or-flight) nervous system. Because it elevates arousal, heart rate, and breathing, stress is useful for helping animals and humans escape dangerous situations, however, it can damage the body to be subjected to stressful conditions for too long.

Get Activated

[Activation code] A stressful event is one that activates your sympathetic (fight-or-flight) nervous system.

STRESSORS

Stressors can come in many forms from immediate physical threats like that of an angry dog, to social threats like an angry friend. In experimental studies in rats, a distinction is often made between social stress and physical stress, but both types activate the hypothalamic-pituitary-adrenal axis or HPA, albeit through different pathways.

The HPA axis is a complex set of direct influences and steroid-producing feedback interactions among the hypothalamus, the pituitary gland, and the adrenal glands. All vertebrates have an HPA, but the steroid-producing stress response is so important that even invertebrates and monocellular organisms have analogous systems.

The HPA is important to psychology because it is intimately involved with many mood disorders involving stress, including anxiety disorder, bipolar disorder, insomnia, PTSD, borderline personality disorder, ADHD, depression, and many others. Antidepressants work by regulating the HPA axis.

It is my aim to help you develop a broader functional understanding of the way that your brain performance directly influences your instinctive or default behavior in reaction to stimuli you are exposed to. With this insight, you will be empowered to consciously choose behavior responses that better serve your intention in any given moment.

LEVERAGING YOUR INSTINCT

The fight-or-flight response (or acute stress response) is a physiological reaction that occurs in response to a perceived harmful event, attack, or threat to survival.

More specifically, the adrenal medulla produces a hormonal cascade that results in the secretion of catecholamines, especially norepinephrine and epinephrine. The hormones estrogen, testosterone, and cortisol, as well as the neurotransmitters dopamine and serotonin, also affect how you react to stress.

THE AUTONOMIC NERVOUS SYSTEM

The autonomic nervous system is a control system that acts largely unconsciously and regulates heart rate, digestion, respiratory rate, pupillary response, urination, and sexual arousal. This system is the primary mechanism in control of the fight-or-flight response and its role is mediated by two different components: the sympathetic nervous system and the parasympathetic nervous system.

THE SYMPATHETIC NERVOUS SYSTEM

The sympathetic nervous system originates in the spinal cord and its main function is to activate the physiological changes that occur during the fight-or-flight response. This component of the autonomic nervous system uses and activates the release of norepinephrine in the reaction.

THE PARASYMPATHETIC NERVOUS SYSTEM

The parasympathetic nervous system originates in the sacral spinal cord and medulla, physically surrounding the sympathetic origin, and works in concert with the sympathetic nervous system. Its main function is to activate the "rest and digest" response and return the body to homeostasis after the fight-or-flight response. This system uses and activates the release of the neurotransmitter acetylcholine.

The reaction begins in the amygdala which triggers a neural response in the hypothalamus. The initial reaction is followed by activation of the pituitary gland and secretion of the hormone ACTH. The adrenal gland is activated almost simultaneously, via the sympathetic nervous system, and releases the hormone epinephrine.

[Activation code] The autonomic nervous system is the primary mechanism in control of the fight-or-flight response, mediated by the sympathetic nervous system and the parasympathetic nervous system.

CHEMICAL MESSENGERS

The release of chemical messengers results in the production of the hormone cortisol, which increases blood pressure, blood sugar, and suppresses the immune system. The initial response and subsequent reactions are triggered in an effort to create a boost of energy. This boost of energy is activated by epinephrine binding to liver cells and the subsequent production of glucose.

The circulation of cortisol also functions to turn fatty acids into available energy, which prepares muscles throughout the body for a response. Catecholamine hormones, such as adrenaline (epinephrine) or noradrenaline (norepinephrine), facilitate immediate physical reactions associated with a preparation for violent muscular action and among others; acceleration of heart and lung action, paling or flushing, or alternating between both, inhibition of stomach and upper-intestinal action to the point where digestion slows down or stops, general effect on the sphincters of the body, constriction of blood vessels in many parts of the body, liberation of metabolic energy sources (particularly fat and glycogen) for muscular action, dilation of blood vessels for muscles, inhibition of the lacrimal gland (responsible for tear production) and salivation, dilation of pupil (mydriasis), relaxation of bladder, inhibition of erection, auditory exclusion (loss of hearing), tunnel vision (loss of peripheral vision), disinhibition of spinal reflexes and shaking.

FUNCTION OF PHYSIOLOGICAL CHANGES

The physiological changes that take place during the fight or flight response are activated in order to give the body increased strength and speed in anticipation of fighting or running. Some of the specific physiological changes and their functions include; increased blood flow to the muscles activated by diverting blood flow from other parts of the body, increased blood pressure, heart rate, blood sugars, and fats in order to supply the body with extra energy.

The blood clotting function of the body speeds up in order to prevent excessive blood loss in the event of an injury sustained during the response. There is an increased muscle tension in order to provide the body with extra speed and strength.

COGNITIVE COMPONENTS - CONTENT SPECIFICITY

The specific components of the mental action or process of acquiring knowledge and understanding in the fight or flight response seem to be largely negative.

These negative cognitions may be characterized by: attention to negative stimuli, the perception of ambiguous situations as negative, and the recurrence of recalling negative words. There also may be specific negative thoughts associated with emotions commonly seen in the reaction.

PERCEPTION OF CONTROL

Perceived control relates to an individual's thoughts about control over situations and events. Perceived control should be differentiated from actual control because an individual's beliefs about their abilities may not reflect their actual abilities. Therefore, overestimation or underestimation of perceived control can lead to anxiety and aggression.

SOCIAL INFORMATION PROCESSING

The social information processing model proposes a variety of factors that determine behavior in the context of social situations and pre-existing thoughts. The attribution of hostility, especially in ambiguous situations, seems to be one of the most important cognitive factors associated with the fight or flight response because of its implications towards aggression.

HOMEOSTASIS

Homeostasis is defined as the maintenance or regulation of the stable condition of an organism and of its internal environment or most simply the balance of bodily functions. Homeostasis is brought about by a natural resistance to change in the optimal conditions, and equilibrium is maintained by many regulatory mechanisms. Your physical body is the most effective mechanism in maintaining homeostasis.

BECOME BODY CONSCIOUS

Your physical body is a tool, a servant if you will, to your mind and your soul. It is the vehicle gifted to you to live out your purpose. It is constantly talking to you through signals however you are blind to them until you become conscious and consenting to hear them.

The problem for most people is that you have become so comfortable and familiar living within your earth suit in its current condition that are not aware of its purpose. It is a little like walking past a magnificent piece of art hanging on a wall. The first time you see the artwork it gets your attention and you might even pause for a moment to take in and appreciate what you see. After a while you may still recognize the picture, even appreciate it as you walk past, however you no longer pause and give it much of your conscious attention.

A few months later and that artwork now hangs on the wall in your house in that same position that you regularly walk past. It is still in your view countless times every day yet you walk past it without giving it too much thought. After a period of time the significance of that artwork becomes lost to you. One could say you no longer consciously see it.

It is still there, in line of sight visible to your naked eye, however, your mind has processed the data as a normal part of the environment you operate in. What was once a beautiful piece of inspiration has now become a dull part of the noise of everyday life.

The incredible creation that is your physical body is often just like that artwork hanging on the wall. You 'walk past it' every day. You see past it in the mirror in the morning. You avoid the glance of the reflection in the window and the shop door. You dance around the silhouette of your shadow in the afternoon. Having become so familiar with your own body your mind has relegated recognizing it to be just a part of the noise.

In this desensitized state your conscious mind can become deaf to the signals that your masterpiece of an earth suite is trying to bring to your attention. One could say that you are running blind as you navigate the world around without the 'insight' that your own earth suite has to offer. And then you wonder why you make poor decisions. You wonder why you find yourself in comprised situations again and again, but it's like you just don't see the signs.

It's important to recognize that your body is not trying to sell you out. You nurture the idea that you have done something wrong or that you are broken in some way, just because you are learning to recognize more accurately how you react in situations. While this is wonderful, that you are seeing yourself in an authentic light, the notion that you are broken will not serve you.

This only creates a negative emotion that you experience as a result of your personal assessment and judgment, which itself is a destructive or negative state. The fact that you experience a physical sensation in your body is a very good thing. Take your time to process how you feel in your physical state.

Learn to recognize the condition of your physiology and indentify the emotion that you have attached to the physical sensation. You can actively and intentionally shift the state that you experience in your physical body at any given time. There are three levers to be able to do this.

The first has to do with acknowledging the condition of your intellectual or mental state. This is the work of recognizing the way your brain allows your mind to operate at any given moment and the impact that it has on your emotion or physical experience in response to a stimulus.

The second has to do with acknowledging the condition of your emotional state. This is the work of recognizing your emotion at any given moment and the impact that they have on the caliber of your thinking and physical activity in response to a stimulus.

The third has to do with acknowledging the condition of your physiological state or body. This is the work of recognizing how you experience sensation in your physical body at any given moment and the impact that has on the way that you feel (emotion) and how that influences the way that you think in response to a stimulus.

Becoming body conscious has to do teaching yourself to become more alert of the state your body is in. You can start by becoming aware of the condition of your physical body. By that, I mean recognizing the level of discomfort that you experience in your major muscle groups. The easiest to learn and recognize and perhaps the most obvious is the sensation of strain in are your neck, shoulders and back.

The physical state of your body has a material impact on the energy state that you nurture and therefore experience at any given moment of time. When you sit or stand in 'healthy' stance, with your spine upright and straight, you allow the muscles of your body function well. This also promotes better flow of blood to the major parts of your body which in turn ensures that you are oxygenated and can function well. This achieved through an improved ability to practice effective breathing which significantly increases your lung capacity.

When you practice poor posture you are effective 'crunching' the life out of your body. Firstly, you significantly compromise your breathing with an arched back and you are effectively compacting your lungs and chest cavity, thereby reducing the potential lung capacity available for to you to take in oxygen.

That is not the only stress you place yourself under with poor posture. With your spine in a compact position, you are placing all related muscle group under additional strain and your body translates this stress further to other muscle groups and body parts

As you develop your ability to practice breathing with a full lung capacity, you will enjoy more effective the dispersion of oxygen across your body and more effective the extraction of impurities, both through your exhale and through the lymphatic and blood systems. The first significant benefit is that of a significant improvement of the energy state that you will experience through your body. The second major benefit will the be state of your mind and the condition of your thinking.

Happiness is the product of the experience of the impact of hormones on our thinking and feeling, intellect and emotion, It can be said to be a sense of sensual gratification that is translated as a positive experience. The key insight here is to understand how our physiological experience and the condition of our thinking can have a material impact on the secretion and behavior of hormones in our body which directly impact your ability to experience a sense of happiness.

THE INSTINCT OVER INTENTION TRAP

As you become more aware of how your mind behaves you will be empowered to practice better caliber thinking. By that I mean you will develop the ability to recognize when your mind is pulling your thinking capacity away from optimal performance intended for you to serve your purpose.

You will be able to 'catch' yourself in a behavioral response before your brain is hijacked by an instinctive reaction. You will develop the ability to actively choose to respond to stimuli and engage with your environment with intentional and deliberate responses.

This is a learned skill. Instinctive behavior is natural and powerful. You could say that it's billions of years strong, however, that does not mean that intentional thinking is not as strong or that it is possible without effort. Only that it will require diligent practice over time and intention with the will to act.

As you expand your working understanding of how your brain and your mind work, you will be less intimidated by the complexity of the organ. With this insight, you will become empowered to take decisive action and better harness the capacity and potential of your brain.

You will need to learn to work through self-limiting beliefs that continuously try to trip you up. You will need to sift through your invisible scripts as you learn to select which self talk to believe and which to discard. You will need to take up courage as you learn to decide for your brain what you will allow your head and heart to focus on.

You will need to give yourself permission to learn to use simple intentional thinking practices. These are not difficult however they will push your mind to exhaustion as they demand that the brain works even harder, forcing it to consume calories. Your body is naturally designed to avoid this so you will have to choose to put into action practices that will help you become more intentional.

DISTRACTED

How often do you catch yourself having become distracted, your thoughts having wandered off in a different direction to that what you were focused on only a moment ago? Perhaps it was triggered by natural curiosity as one creative thought leads to the birth of a hundred alternative new possibilities. Often it can be something as simple as a noticing a similar but contrasting idea and your attention is pulled into an entirely new direction. This it is the time to #GetActivated.

SLUGGISH / SLOW

Notice how your thinking become sluggish or slow and it feels like there is a soft mist or cloud hanging around your mind that constrains your ability to think clearly. It's not that you cannot 'see' well in the moment but rather that you have lost the edge to your thinking.

When it feels like it is taking longer than normal for your thoughts to connect, for ideas to take shape and for you to come to conclusions then is time to #GetActivated.

DOUBTFUL / QUESTIONING YOURSELF

Perhaps you may find that you are taking a long time to make a decision to act, that you're hesitating but you are not clear why. This it is the time to #GetActivated.

LIMITING BELIEFS

The real reason why most of us are 'trapped' in a particular pattern of behavior has to do with a set of beliefs that constrain us in some way, often referred to as self-limiting beliefs. The interesting aspect about this is that you don't have to actively or intentionally think them, or even do anything about a set of thoughts, they none the less have a significant impact on our lives. This is the time to #GetActivated.

Even more so just by the mere fact that you have established a particular belief, it has the power to shape and guide how you think and in turn what you will or will not do or say. In this way, a set of limiting beliefs has a significant and material impact on your life. Yet most of the time you do not even see or realize it.

[Activation code] The real reason most of us are 'trapped' in a particular pattern of behavior has to do with a set of beliefs that constrain us in some way.

Why is that? Well, you have many beliefs, about your rights, duties and responsibilities. You have a set of internal thoughts about what you can and cannot or should and should not do. These thoughts have a deeply embedded emotion attached to them. The stronger that sense of emotion, the more you perceive that thought or idea to be real. So real you assume these thoughts to be part of a universal truth. The stronger the emotion so much more your mind and heart accept it to make up a part of your identity of self.

One way that you can recognize if you are subject to these kinds of self-limiting belief is to identify if you use personal definition statements as part of your regular language. They are formulated as the "I am ..", "I will .." , "I can .." or "I can not .. " phrases.

I AM / I DO

When most people introduce themselves on the first encounter, they use a short set of descriptions to describe who they believe they are. Often they define themselves by what they do or do not do.

"I am an engineer" is a telling description of one's profession and practice however it does not tell me much about your character or personality. You leave the rest up to me to assume, perhaps because you yourself have a set of assumptions about what kind of person an engineer is.

I CAN / I CAN'T

Somewhere in that description of practicing as an engineer is an idea of what you believe you can and what you can't do. Some of it has to do with your talents and abilities that you have shaped over time into your capabilities while the rest is a set of laws and rules about what a person who is qualified in a particular profession may or may not do.

I often hear people extend their own ideas of what it means to be a professional onto a title like this. For example, you might assume that all engineers are intelligent people with a very high IQ. It would make sense to you that this kind of person acts in a particular way both at work and at home.

However, having a high IQ does not determine your preference, say as to how you like to pack your cupboards or how neat you keep your car.

I MUST / I MUST NOT

As you buy into a particular set of beliefs, you may also subscribe to a set of values and behavioral norms associated to them. These are a little less rigid than rules and laws however they are still prescriptive in how you believe you are allowed to think and then behave.

Often these beliefs are never verbalized however very active in your thought life. They are the internal conversation that you have with yourself about the actions that you feel that you must take. More often than not the internal conversation is filled up with unspoken statements about what actions you feel and therefore believe you are not supposed or even allowed to do.

If you find that you are a 'driven' person who is never at rest you may recognize that you have subscribed to a set of beliefs about what you feel you 'must do'. Many of these are closely related to the shaping characters you were exposed to in our your youth like that of your mother and father.

I AM / AM NOT

There is a powerful force that you have chosen to subject yourself to in that you subscribed to the verb 'to be'. It has a defining or shaping power in that it influences how you define yourself. If you say to yourself that you are one thing, the logic of your subconscious mind will try to convince you that are not another.

If you say of yourself that you are an engineer, your logical mind will actively try and convince you that you are not an artist. If you say that you are a strong person, especially as a leader-manager, the same thinking will work at convincing you that you cannot also be a soft or tender person. This kind of thinking is a typical self-limiting belief.

WHAT STATE ARE YOU IN?

DOES YOUR EMOTIONAL STATE SERVE YOU?

When we are successful, we will help you develop the ability to check in on a regular basis. Check in to what you may ask? Your emotional state and the impact it has on the caliber of your thinking and behavior response at any given moment.

The second part of this book was about developing a working understanding of your brain chemistry and the impact that it has on your emotional thinking. The way that you feel about what you are thinking about is central to recognizing an opportunity to #Get Activated.

As you recognize that emotions are energy-in-motion you can begin to see how energy can be either serving you towards or disrupting you from optimal performance and the ability to live in your purpose.

IDENTIFY INTENTIONAL RESPONSES

With this level of insight, you can begin to identify layers of intentional responses that you can choose to activate at any given moment in the context of the environment you are in. With an activated awareness you can develop the ability to recognize the state of your energy, as experienced in an emotion, in relation to the environment you are in. By that, I mean that the energy state that you experience in your physical body is a result of processing a set of stimuli in the context of the environment that you find yourself in.

Your experience of any given stimulus will be processed in the three domains of your intellectual, emotional and physiological sense-making capacity. While the trigger may sit in any one of these domains, they each have an impact on your overall energy state and therefore your chosen behavior response in the situation.

INDENTIFY THE TRIGGER

To learn to take advantage of this, you must identify the trigger that has had the most significant impact on your current energy state. In our framework, we will consider one of three domains to make sense of the stimulus that you can give attention to. The important thing to remember is that the stimulus is not the problem that you are working on, rather your chosen response to it.

The Activated intelligence (Ai) framework describes the domain of your intellectual intelligence or Head Sense, the domain of your emotional intelligence or Heart Sense and the domain of your physiological intelligence of body sense which for the sake of alliteration we refer to as the Hand Sense.

In short I talk about the Head-Heart-Hand model (or H3). This is an abbreviated way of describing how you (intellectually) think, (emotionally) feel and (physically) act in any given moment. While you will process stimuli quite differently in each H3 domain, and you could say that they operate separately, it is also important to note that they do not work in isolation. If there is any magic sauce to the Ai framework and the H3 model it is this.

As you put your Ai awareness to practice you will develop the ability to become mindful in which H3 domain a stimulus caused a trigger that has now influenced your response and directed your behavior. Again the key is not to address the behavior. The opportunity that your Ai awareness creates is to intervene at your trigger response and learn how to intentionally select your desired response behavior.

MAKE THE SHIFT DESIRED

Consider the state of your thinking and how has it served you to engage in your optimal performance abilities. If you have ever been in one of the classrooms where I train you would hear me say that "your stinking was thinking for you". As a result of the poor state of thinking that you chose to respond with you denied yourself the opportunity to use the most appropriate intellectual response to process that particular stimulus.

WORKING 'UPWARDS'

While it is not a rule of law for the most part you may find it easiest to recognize triggers to stimuli in the emotional domain (or Heart sense). Keep in mind that for most people you can best 'experience' your emotional state (Heart sense) when you allow yourself to become aware of what your (Hand sense) body is 'feeling' as it processes the stimuli you are exposed to through your physiology.

My experience has taught me to consider the body (Hand Sense) perception as an indication of the emotional experience (Heart sense) that I have chosen to translate from the encounter. This is then a helpful pointer to consider the caliber of thinking (Head Sense) that I have used to create meaning which has supported the emotional interpretation of the physical experience in response to the stimulus.

The opportunity this presents is that you are able to 'work upwards' and address the mental model and mind state that you have cultivated that allowed the condition to persist, both of which you have the ability to influence.

By that I mean that you can develop the ability to influence the mind state that your cognition and executive functions operate in. You can intentionally influence and therefore change the operating condition of your brain.

As you elevate your executive function you are better able to influence the mental models that you use to process the environment you are in. These are the reference frameworks that you use to interpret the stimulus and make sense of the response experience.

WORKING 'DOWNWARDS'

In a similar way you can develop the ability to recognize triggers to stimuli in the Head sense or intellectual domain.

As you put these principles into practice you will develop the ability to recognize the caliber of thinking that you are using to make sense of your experience in relation to a set of stimuli.

READY FOR A CHANGE WITHIN

Quite in the face of years of conventional medicine and the well-meaning intentions of good people, I tried something that I had previously held to be taboo.

And it worked. Amazingly well. And it still does. That created some much relief and joy in my physical body but it also created a significant problem. I am referring to my journey to identify and heal the real causes of my long-standing suffering of the symptoms from rhinitis.

When there is not enough evidence to validate a seemingly rational or conventional external explanation, you might then be forced to consider an alternative. Like me, you might be given an opportunity to make a change on the inside. This may be the only way that you find yourself truly considering a significant conversion to set aside a cluster of deeply held beliefs and values, many of which in fact do not serve you well.

The problem is you cannot just be told how to heal yourself or simply decide to follow through on the thoughts and ideas that leaders and gurus have told you. The fact is that other people's ideas, like many sophisticated persuasion techniques, either fail or fail to have permanent changes on an individual. The question is why?

If you really want to experience lasting change, then you must be allowed to create an environment or condition in which you have the opportunity to make the desired shift 'by and for yourself.' Knowing that you should make a change or even knowing how to do it is not enough.

Having the rational understanding does not mean that you have the willpower to embark on the journey or more importantly the energetic technology to make the desired change. This is why I could hold on to a set of (intellectual) beliefs despite the (physical) evidence for so long.

FEEL IT TO BELIEVE IT

It is not enough to have a rational conviction about something that you want to change. You have to learn how to feel it. You will need to learn how to create the experience of inconsistency.

By that I mean, you will need to give yourself permission to go through the physical sensation of experiencing one truth in your body while wrestling with a different intellectual truth in your mind. At times you may even feel like you are at war with yourself, but this is a good thing. This is how you cultivate authenticity and truth. This is the birthplace of deep and sustainable healing and wellbeing.

Often it will take the acute experience of inconsistency between what you think you believe and what you discover you are truly feeling, through physical sensation and your emotional experience. It is in the space between the stale perception of old conditioned belief and newly found conscious awareness that you can stumble onto insights that help you find clarity and understanding about who you really are. More importantly about who you might become if you choose to act on the insights.

This war within then provides the motive inspired force that can propel you into meaningful action. The greater the inconsistency, the greater the tension you experience and the greater the motive to re-discover your personal truth.

This war within can play out in a few ways. You may find that you wrestle with feelings of confusion and uncertainty. Quite often people wrestling through the war within experience dissonance in every area of their life yet are unable to identify its cause. So they rather practice denial and spend a lot of energy defending their irritable condition and negative behavior towards the world around them.

On the other hand, when you are willing to embrace the war within you can experience a new measure of consistency long before you have actually won the battle. You can unlock into your circumstance the feeling of calm, a sensation of balance emerging, of things beginning to run smoothly.

Without actually having all the answers at your fingertips, more and more things begin to go right for you. It is as if you life begins to even out and fall into place if only just a little. But it's a noticeable little that starts to have a significant impact on every other aspect in your life.

Something magical is about to happen. Yet there is something is keeping you from facing up to your own inconsistency and getting the breakthrough you are really looking for.

The longer you keep this war within a secret to yourself, as if no one else really knows about it, the longer you keep yourself trapped inside the walls of your stale set of old beliefs set in place by conditioned thinking. Don't get me wrong, I am not trying to challenge whether the beliefs that you hold to are true or not. All I am asking you to consider at this moment is if they truly serve you.

The challenge with speaking out and asking questions is that you will do exactly that. You will challenge those who are not willing to face up to their own war within. Perhaps even worse, you will come up against people who know different yet want you to stay stuck in the silent trap of your stale beliefs. It is just safer for them that way.

In that way, they can continue to manipulate your thinking and control your behavior, even if only to safeguard their own way of life. They will discourage you from speaking up and go to great lengths to prevent you from speaking out, particularly in public.

It's just not worth it. To stay stuck in your silent cage. Especially when you already have everything you need to break free. It can start with simply giving yourself permission to ask. Pick up courage and give yourself the opportunity to connect with people who you can engage with. People you feel you can trust, who are already outside your old boundaries of belief.

Take up opportunities to act outside your old set of stale standards, those that in truth have only ever hidden the inconsistency between what you believe and how you behave. Reach out to people who already demonstrate that they are making sense of their inconsistency and learning to live life with more consistency with their actions.

CHANGING HABITS

Know that creating this kind of change in your behavior will take time. More importantly when you challenged by a behavior that you would like to see change remember that it is only a learned response. The way in which you conduct yourself is a direct function of your beliefs and values.

In the context of this conversation values are those notions that you hold to be most important to you. The best way I have found to describe a belief is that it is simply a strong emotional conviction about something. That means in any given moment you will select how you think, how you feel and how you conduct yourself in response to a set of stimuli all based on what you feel is most important to you.

When you do this repeatedly over a period of time the selected conduct becomes a habit. Given enough reinforcement this habit then shapes your behavior. Over the course of our life your behaviors will govern 'the way you do things' and shape your culture. Your culture then is what keeps your beliefs strong and in place.

In practice, we now know that you can intentionally increase a particular desired habit by:
- Doing it more often.
- Connecting it with a stimulus that happens often.
- Making the reward more pleasurable.
- Making each enacting of the habit more powerful.
- Doing it for longer each time.

But wait just a minute if habits are increased and deepened by repetition then it goes to say that the power of a habit can be broken relatively simply by removing the stimulus or alternatively by interrupting the habit response as it is being enacted. Yes, I know, simple does not mean easy.

CREATING CHANGE

A vital key to creating change lies in identifying the moment that you engage your mental process to select what you think, feel or experience. This is called cognitive arousal where the rational thinking is wakened to find a justification for an action or event.

If you want to be able to change your habits, you will need to learn how to intentionally think with the full range of your senses so that you can make a rational argument for the inconsistencies you will experience.

You will need to learn how to engage cognitive arousal as you stand up to the war that wages within.

CULTIVATING CURIOSITY

One way you can make this possible is through cultivating curiosity and interest. Curiosity is the desire to learn more, to discover interesting or useful facts. It seeks to complete understanding, to assess threats and explore opportunities.

Interest is both fascination in the moment and a general interest in particular topics. To grow your curiosity, give yourself permission to hint at possibility rather than accept everything on face value. You can keep interest alive by allowing a constant stream of new information that promises to help you meet needs and achieve goals drip into your awareness.

TEND TO TENSION

Resolving outstanding tensions shows value in cognitive arousal. If you can create or recognize the 'aha' of learning or the 'hurrah' of problems solved then you will experience the positive energy of gratitude. Tensions aroused create cognitive motivation. Resolving this kind of tension creates space (and permission) for more. Cognitive tensions include problems, puzzles and philosophical thoughts. Think about the way that you feel when discover that you can provide an answer to a challenge or problem.

FINDING FLOW

When you get really involved in what you are doing, you can enter a state of 'flow'. In this state, it is easy to lose track of time and self. And when you come back to yourself there is often a strong sense of enjoyment and fulfillment. You can create more opportunity to experience flow by engaging with challenge situations that you feel you have enough confidence to solve. These should not be too difficult. Make sure you have enough time and resources but at the same time it should not be so easy that you totally relax.

Cognitive arousal is particularly helpful when you want to learn how to make a permanent change of mind. Keep this in mind when you consider a rational argument for an inconsistency you experience. Your personal conclusions are more likely to stick with your change over the longer term when you have intentionally engaged all your senses to apply careful thought to the change process.

THE ACTIVATED INTELLIGENCE TRIFECTA

So you want to change your mind about things. You have had enough of the way that you typically respond in particular situations. Perhaps you are ready to recognize that your behavior doesn't serve you anymore and something just has to shift. You are ready to take back control of your circumstances and make some serious changes. More importantly you realize now that you just have to. And no one else will do it for you. So now is the time. If you were waiting for a sign, this is it.

The starting place to apply this guide to help you make the necessary shift is to learn to recognize which set of circumstances you are ready to work into. Where is that? You know, usually the situations in which you find yourself most often behave 'that' way.

It might come out in aggressive behavior, perhaps a more subtle passive aggression. It could be that moment when you find yourself shouting out at someone at the top of your voice but you have no idea how it escalated to that so quickly. On the other hand it could be another one of those moments which you only recognize in retrospect that you held back on your power and have somehow learned to retract into your shell. Perhaps you did not mean to go into hiding but now you realize that you have, and you can see that it isn't serving you.

Whether it is an obvious behavior that is difficult to hide or one so subtle that you conveniently do not notice it, your journey to becoming activated begins by recognizing that you allow yourself to become subject to a set of stimuli. Left unattended you will continue to give your power to the behavior response that you have associated with the stimulus which you are regularly exposed to.

A stimulus will fulfill the role of a trigger. It sets off a sequence of events which affects your state which in turn pulls you toward a set of learned responses. These responses are typically conditioned or automatic behaviors. They create a set of default or instinctive reactions, your behavioral traits that seem to result without you having to give much thought to them. They are not bound only to the physical body but include your intellectual and emotional behavior.

[Activation code] A stimulus will trigger a sequence of events which pull you toward a set of learned responses that are typically conditioned (or learned) or automatic behaviors.

The hardest work is really done when you give yourself permission to recognize the stimulus that has triggered your undesirable behavior. The easiest to discern is usually the incident that takes place in the physical domain. This could be something as simple as feeling frustrated by the distraction caused by noise introduced in your working environment. It can also be as basic as getting your finger caught in the door.

Let's chat a little about that noise. What I want you to hear me say is that it's not the actual sound that has been introduced into the environment that creates the problem. The fact is that the noise is just waves of energy. They cannot do damage or really hurt you while you sit there at your desk. Yet something happens and before you know it you have lost your concentration. That noise interruption seems to steal your energy and your ability to focus on your work. Your concentration is broken and you experience a shift in your behavior as your move away from a state of peace to experience the sensation of stress.

When you become clear about the actual trigger you have selected to respond to, you can also step into your power as you are now positioned to do something about it. Again it's not so much about the trigger. It is all about that fact that a stimulus in your environment has triggered a change in your behavior, that you have selected a particular emotion related response. This response is driven by a value or motive that you consider to be under threat leading you to experience the sensation of stress. It can just the same be a motive of good that you are aligned to. In that case, your behavior response will be as convincing but positive.

Get Activated

> [Activation code] Again it's not so much about the trigger but that a stimulus in your environment has triggered a change in your behavior and that you have chosen a particular response.

Take, for example, the moment you realized that your concentration was broken by the noise interruption. Perhaps the real issue, when you felt that you lost your concentration as a result of the noise, is that you lost your sense of control. You might feel that your ability to complete your task or achieve the desire outcome is at threat. In that moment you allow yourself to shift from a state of flow into a condition where you experience stress.

It is this stress of the perceived potential loss that is the real issue. It is the stress sensation that triggers a sequence of events that lead to you display an undesired conduct. It is this set of behaviors that you now try to justify. But why is it that something so simple like a little uninvited noise can have such a strong influence on your behavior? So much so that before you know it you catch yourself displaying behavior that you quickly come to regret.

It is because the sensation you experience triggered by that stimulus has threatened a value or belief that is important to you. When you recognize that you are struggling to concentrate you experience the sensation of losing control of the situation. This is what sets a course of emotionally charged behavioral acts in motion. Before you can catch yourself you might react aggressively by raising your voice to shout at someone or perhaps even throw something across the room.

This reaction to the sensation of loss of control sets in motion a sequence of events that take place through your body. They are the direct result of the secretion of hormones and chemicals that are rapidly transferred through your blood. These stimulate the tissues and cells of your body into action. However, they have consequences, many of which you are oblivious to.

> [Activation code] It is because the experience triggered by that stimulus has threatened a value or belief that is important to you.

Some of these hormones act as neurotransmitters transmitting vital information to and from your brain. They rapidly influence the way your physiology behaves.

Cortisol is a hormone best known for the role that it plays in the "fight-or-flight" response. It stimulates the body to focus on processes that are essential for immediate survival. Adrenaline plays an important role in increasing blood flow to your muscles. Noradrenalin mobilizes the brain and gets your body ready to take action. Norepinephrine increases arousal and alertness and helps you focus your attention. Adrenaline can also increase restlessness and anxiety.

Dopamine is used to help regulate your gross motor behavior and helps improve your working memory. It promotes feelings of pleasure and makes you select actions that lead to pleasure and emotional arousal. The secretion of

Get Activated

Serotonin helps to regulate the endorphins that increase your sense of well-being and improve your humor.

Your physical body responds rapidly under the influence of these hormones influencing the way that you think and then feel. If you are repeatedly exposed to a similar stimulus, you can learn to recognize the regular behavior response that is undesirable. The same trigger will elicit a similar emotion related action as the associated action is part of a conditioned or learned response linked to the particular stimulus. Over time this becomes a habit and then your behavior.

[Activation code] Your physical body responds rapidly under the influence of the hormones influencing the way that you think and feel.

This similar repeated action becomes your instinctive go-to response every time you are triggered by the same stimulus. As you learn to effectively associate the offending behavior to the particular stimulus you will be in a position to dismantle the power that the trigger has over your behavior.

More importantly you will be able to open a window of opportunity to create shift. You can widen that window by learning to actively process the experience in the moment that you recognize you have been triggered. The key is to identify the active stimulus so that you can determine by which domain you have been drawn to an emotion related behavioral response.

In the case of the noise stimulus I submit that the most probable trigger response would reside in your physiological domain. As the trigger sensation increases you experience more difficulty on focus your attention. When you run out of capacity to regulate your emotional response to the physical experience that has been triggered you react and display the offending behavior.

The same stimulus can also elicit a trigger response that resides in your intellectual domain. As the trigger sensation increases you experience dissonance in your mental condition causing you to move out of flow as you find it more difficult to focus your attention and concentrate. Eventually your mind succumbs to the physical brain muscle fatigue of focusing in response to regulating the emotion created by the tension.

Another form of fatigue on your intellectual domain is when your mind state, that is the operating condition of your brain, no longer supports optimal cognitive abilities and your caliber of mental processing deteriorates. In the simplest terms your "think" begins to "stink". The trigger may elicit a set of responses that are rooted in a set of principles that 'force' you to display the offending behavior. This behavior is then an expression of the mental model or philosophy that you are invested in, one demanding behavior that does not serve your purpose or intention well at that moment.

The same stimulus can elicit a trigger response in your emotional state. As the trigger sensation increases you pass an inflection point where your executive function and mental processing are hijacked by emotion. This takes place when you experience an amygdale hijack and your fight-or-flight response is activated. You will find yourself trying to modify the situation around you so as to minimize the emotional impact of your experience.

Remember that your RAS will act as a filter to illuminate out unnecessary information so that only what you perceive to be most relevant gets through. It will take what you focus on and actively create a filter for it, sifting through the data and presenting only the pieces that you feel are important to you.

> [Activation code] Remember that your RAS will act as a filter so that only what you perceive to be most relevant gets through.

You need to recognize that your mind is wired to seek out and present information that validates your beliefs. It filters your experience of the world through the parameters YOU give it. Your values and beliefs shape those parameters. In this way, the RAS 'helps' you see what you really want to see. This takes place on a subconscious or invisible level, and in doing so influences your actions without you noticing it. In one sense we can say that you can be blinded by your own beliefs.

> [Activation code] This takes place on a subconscious level influencing your actions without you even noticing it. In one sense we can say that you can be blinded by your own beliefs.

This is why when you are ready to make those necessary changes it is vital that you take the time to apply this level of mental processing to your trigger experience. This includes processing your feelings (emotion), thoughts (thinking), emotion-related (sensation) physiological responses and your emotion-driven behavior (actions).

When you apply this level of rational thought you can sift through the camouflage of emotion-related responses and establish what is truly important to you. These are the things that you value most. These are the things that you will find you are instinctively wired to safeguard and protect.

This is your most significant insight when you can recognize the behavior that you display free of the emotion that clouds your rational thought and sees it for what it is. When you can see what you value most and how your behavior is conditioned to protect that, even when that behavior does not serve your intention in the present moment.

This is when the inconsistency that you experience will become plain to see. This is when you can begin to make informed decisions about the choices you make and how you respond to your emotion. This is how you can consciously change your behavior and co-create a more desirable future.

With the new-found insight uncovered by decoding your inconsistency, you can begin to select a more appropriate action response to associate with the trigger. In this state of conscious awareness, you are able to take back full control of your mental processes in the situation. You become empowered to select a more appropriate emotionally related

Get Activated

response and then identify which value you will chose to defend in that context going forward.

> [Activation code] This includes processing your feelings (emotion), thoughts (thinking), emotion-related (sensation) physiological responses and your emotion-related behavior (actions).

To do that, you will need to learn to engage all your senses by intentionally using the Ai trifecta. The key to leveraging the benefit of the Ai trifecta lies in developing the ability to extract real-time insight from all three domains of the H3 model, that of your intellectual state (head sense), your emotional state (heart sense) and your body or physiological state (hand sense). I refer to this as the head-heart-hand (H^3) triad.

The important thing to know is that it's not enough to be able to respond with insights from only one domain. You need all three levels of insight in play to activate the benefit of the Ai trifecta. If you do not employ all three insights together you can unintentionally counteract the full benefit of what you might have gained from the influence of just one domain. In effect, you end up working against yourself.

When you have learned how implement the Activated Intelligence Trifecta you will in any given moment be able to:
- Consider the *situation you are in.
- Identify the *stimulus that you has triggered you.
- Acknowledge the *response that it is pulling you to.

- Accept the set of *beliefs that do not serve you.
- Recognize the *behavior that is sabotaging you.
- Establish the *value and what is important to you.
- Engage *cognitive arousal and apply *rational thought.
- Regulate your *emotional related responses.
- Consciously select an *intentional H^3 response.
- *Reinforce the desired behavior across the H^3 triad.

This is the deliberate intersection of an activated mind or intellectual intelligence, an activated heart or emotional intelligence and an activated body or physiological intelligence.

Just a note: Why do I refer to the physiological domain as 'hand(s)'? Well, it is simply because in the arena of professional development and corporate training the solution that is introduced needs to be a pragmatic one. By that I mean you will need to be able to do something tangible with what we teach you. More often than not a successful behavior change solution will be something that can be translated into simple action that you can take. In most cases, and particularly when we work closer to the front line of an organization, that simple action will require your hands to take action and empower you to conduct a task more effectively.

GET ACTIVATED – HABITS OF THE ACTIVATED LIFE

In my earlier work on cracking the common sense code, I found that it is often easier to describe what something isn't than to simply define what it is. In one sense it is easier to recognize and point out when someone does not demonstrate common sense than it is to teach that same individual how to develop it. We can apply the same observation to the conversation of developing your ability to demonstrate the Activated H3 habits that empower you to leverage the Ai trifecta.

In most cases, the kind of people who I get to work with are already open to personal development. Perhaps you have already taken the step to begin your journey towards personal mastery. That includes learning to open your mind to improving the state of your cognitive abilities.

You are willing to recognize that somehow you have allowed yourself to become obstructed from achieving the desired result. This is because of emotion-related decisions that you have made about your behavior have to lead you to respond in a way that does not serve your intention or allow you to achieve the outcomes you were aiming for.

This obstruction can be experienced as a sensation of frustration or disappointment. Do you recall the earlier example of a noise introduced into your working environment? Remember that the issue is not the sound that introduced as a disturbance but rather the effect that you allow it to have on your thinking, feeling and behavior.

With the disturbance, you lose your level of concentration and your ability to focus on your work is undermined. Again, neither of these are the issue at hand. The real problem is the anxiety you experience as a result of the situation. The lack of focus and loss of concentration have a direct impact on your productivity. This can create an impression that your workload will increase and with it the time pressure to complete your task.

These create a feeling of anxiety. In a manner of seconds, you experience a fear of the possible consequences, you experience a sense of loss and you develop a concern for how you will deal with it all. As your mind processes this your body already releases a cascade of hormones as we have described earlier, each with their impact on the operation condition of your body.

In quite a natural manner your physical body responds to the presence of hormones and you become aware of the physical sensation of the tightening of your chest and 'butterflies' in your stomach. As the sudden rush of increased adrenaline races through your blood during the fight-flight response, you may experience an acute amygdala hijack and a temporary loss of control of your rational thought and conscious thinking.

In that moment the average person will most likely just do nothing. You hesitate. You freeze. A few moments later you find yourself practicing your procrastination skills as you feel stuck again in the spiral of distraction or in-action. Does this scenario sound familiar? A better question to ask is what could you learn to look out for so that you don't find yourself trapped in this cycle again?

You can develop the ability to recognize the obstruction. The truth is that we are creatures of habit and are often tripped up by the same obstruction. This is a good thing in so much that when you can see the patterns in which you allow yourself to be triggered by an obstruction you can become better prepared to deal with them.

There is also a pattern or behavior script in the way that you choose to respond to those triggers. Again the good news is that you can unlearn them.

ENGAGE YOUR ACTIVATION STRATEGY

There are five systematic steps that you can consciously follow as you take deliberate action to put the Activated H^3 habits into practice and fast track a change to the script of your learned behavior response.

1. Identify the obstruction
2. Recognize the trigger
3. Acknowledge the H3 domain
4. Execute the shift strategy > activation tactic
5. Integrate across the triad

Get Activated | Step One: Identify The Obstruction

Your first move is to identify what is actually going on in the context of the situation that you find yourself in. Give particular attention to the circumstance so that you can separate that what you experience with your emotions from that what you feel in your body.

You want to be able to describe the situation by the events that have taken place separate from the emotion you have experienced from each individual occurrence. This will help you identify the particular stimulus that you have allowed to obstruct you from your purpose or intention.

When we described the example of the uninvited noise earlier you will have recognized that your initial awareness was when you noticed that you had lost your focus and could no longer concentrate effectively. After applying some thought you came to realize that your first conscious awareness was actually when recognized the sensation of frustration. While you had now become aware of a change in your behavior in the form of the sensation of frustration it was only a consequence of the obstruction, which was, in this case, the loss of focus. This change in behavior has now become an obstruction to fulfilling your purpose or intention at that moment.

Get Activated | Step Two: Recognize The Trigger

Next, you will need to recognize in the simplest form possible where you have experienced the sensory trigger. By that I mean to identify the emotion that you have associated with the obstruction that occurred.

Recognize the emotion-related response that you have chosen to perform, that is your current behavior. At this stage, it's not about whether this conduct is right or wrong, good or bad. It is about comprehending what is going on so that you can develop a rational sense about the cause of your behavior response. This will also help you to see that you are in fact conducting yourself in accordance with your personal behavior script as defined and dictated by your values and beliefs. This is where you might begin to recognize how some of your current beliefs, like those about your self-identity and self-worth, do not serve you well.

The obstruction in our example is identified as the sound that caused the interruption and led to the breakdown of your focus and concentration. The sensory trigger in that event was the anxiety elicited as a learned emotional response to the expectation of a perceived loss of control. The sound was never the real issue however it caused a trigger that leads to a change in your behavior and the shift in state from experiencing flow to that of stress. You will need to learn to identify the emotion of sensory triggers that you can focus your effort correctly.

Get Activated | Step Three: Acknowledge The H3 Domain Response

You will need to be able to express in the simplest words possible exactly what you are experiencing as a result of the emotion elicited by the sensory trigger. This will require that you process your feelings (emotions), consider your thoughts (thinking), get in touch with your physiological (sensation) response and unpack your emotion-related behavior (actions).

Give yourself permission to acknowledge from which H3 domain you are processing the trigger and selecting your primary emotion-related behavior response. You must establish whether you are justifying your choice to react in this way based on a value that you hold to in your thinking, an emotional feeling you experience in your heart or on a physiological feeling you experience as a condition of your physical body.

In our example, the frustration of the breakdown in ability to concentrate was fueled by the sense of loss of control and the perceived impact that would have on the result of your efforts and the ability to enjoy the outcome you had been aiming for. The sensory trigger was therefore based in the emotional domain. To deal with the incident effectively you will have to use your heart sense to activate an intentional shift in your emotional domain.

Get Activated | Step Four: Execute A Shift Strategy - The Activation Tactic

Now you are ready to engage cognitive arousal, apply your rational thinking and intentionally select how you can respond differently in the trigger domain.

To activate a shift in the Head domain:
- Consider your thoughts. Is there something about the caliber and condition of your thinking that allows you to be subject to the sensory trigger?
- Would it serve you to consider making an adjustment to your mental model about the situation?

To activate a shift in your Heart domain:
- Consciously process your feelings experienced in the situation.
- Is there something about the situation that is attached to or reminds you of a certain emotion that allows you to be subject to the sensory trigger?
- Would it serve you to revisit the original event or earliest memory of your experience of that emotion and process possible trapped energy or self determining beliefs?

To activate a shift in the Hand domain:
- Actively get in touch with your physiological sensation.
- Is there a logical reason for the condition of your body that allows you to respond in this physical manner?
- For example, do you get enough sleep or are you suffering from physical fatigue? Would you be better able to regulate your emotion if you were sleeping more and experiencing less fatigue?

This is the activation tactic, a deliberate behavior response that you choose to implement as a counterstroke to the obstruction that will alter the impact of the sensory trigger.

Get Activated | Step Five: Integrate Across The H³ Triad

When you can quickly identify ways to take deliberate action to counteract your sensory trigger, you are ready to unlock the true power of this process and integrate your shift strategy further in the other H³ domains.

This is where all other processes fall short in that they do not support you to translate the conscious awareness and behavior change you have achieved in one domain across to the other two. This is how you can leverage the influence of the Ai trifecta and fast track your behavior change.

Consider the activation tactic you have just implemented to create shift in step 4. What simple action can you take reinforce this shift in another Activated H3 domain?

For example, what can you do in the physiological domain to reinforce heart sense shift from anxiety back to a sense of flow? To start you can adjust your breathing so that you have the physical ability to regulate your emotion more effectively. There are also time management tactics and practical concentration tools that you can deploy to help you get your focus back. A simple example is to use the pomodoro technique to better manage your time. If you spend a lot of time working on the computer you can use an app on your phone or on the desktop to help you set up work intervals of 25-minute segments with a 5-minute break before re-engaging in the deep or focused work session again.

What can you do in the intellectual domain to support the heart sense shift back to confidence and a state of flow? The most powerful tactic I recommend in my coaching practice is to revisit your intention for the particular work session. Remind yourself of your 'big why' by revisiting your affirmations or your incantation for the day.

What can you do in the emotional domain to support the head sense shift back to a state of flow? If I was in the room with you, I would ask you to speak out aloud the choice you have made in the intellectual domain. Perhaps it's a different perspective on the situation or choosing a new self talk to speak over the situation. Usually, it will include the "I am" phrase. The key then is to consider how this new thought will make you feel. I want you to get in touch with the sense of the emotion attached to the new thought or language. This positive emotion is the energy that will help you materialize a new context in your situation and support the shift towards the trigger.

DEVELOPING THE ACTIVATED H3 HABITS

As you learn to implement these 5 steps more effectively you will develop the ability to reshape your behavior and put into practice the habits of someone who lives the Activated H3 life.

HABITS OF THE ACTIVATED MIND

Learn how to select the most appropriate intellectual response required for your desired state.

Get Activated

This is the practice of catching your thoughts so that you can govern them to stay in the energetic state that best serves your intention and focused activity.

Activation prompt:

What can you deliberately do to strengthen your Head Sense?
Practice 1: What caliber of thinking am I relying on to make sense of the situation I am in?

- Do you have a simple understanding of your mental models?
- How do you become more aware of your choice of paradigm and the influence on your rational and decision-making abilities?
- Can you describe what you believe is right in the situation?
- Can you explain why that is important to you?
- Can you recognize how your current thinking positively serves your intention and purpose?
- How can you become more alert to the state (energy) of your thinking?
- How can you become more conscious of the condition (accuracy) of your thinking?

What are your activation thieves, the intellectual practices that deliberately sabotage your Head Sense?

- Do you engage in self-defeating self-talk?
- Do you have a set of affirmations of incantations that you revisit on a regular basis?

HABITS OF THE ACTIVATED HEART

Learn how to select the most appropriate emotional response required for your desired state.

This is the practice of recognizing your sensory experience related to the situation so that you can govern your emotions to stay in the energetic state that best serves your intention and purpose.

Activation prompt:

What can you deliberately do to strengthen your Heart Sense? Practice 2: What is the primary emotion that I am experiencing in this situation?

- Can you accurately describe the emotion that you experience as a result of the way that you feel in your physical body and intellectual state in a particular situation?
- Note this is different from how you feel in your body or what you think in your mind.

What are your activation thieves, the emotional practices that deliberately sabotage your Heart Sense?

- Do regularly schedule time for prayer, meditation or contemplation?

HABITS OF THE ACTIVATED BODY

Learn how to select the most appropriate physiological response required that will empower you to show up in your desired (energetic) state.

This is the practice of catching your physiology or body response so that you can govern it to generate the level of energy which enables you to behave in the way that best serves your intentions.

Activation prompt:

What can you deliberately do to strengthen your Hand Sense? Practice 3: What is the condition of my physical body that has the most significant impact on the state that I bring to this situation?

- Do you treat your body to a healthy diet and enough rest?
- Do you drink enough water during the day?
- Do you engage in activities that encourage movement and at least a moderate level of fitness?

What are your activation thieves, the physiological practices that deliberately sabotage your Hand Sense?

- Are you currently sleep deprived or experience physical fatigued?
- Do you rely on caffeine or other stimulants to regulate or enhance your energy levels?

When you are successful, you will be able to make the shift from been trapped by your age-old instinctive reactions, those learned responses that do not match your intention, to reconditioning your thinking to intentionally select intellectual, emotional and physiological behavior responses that help you unlock desirable outcomes that serve your purpose.

In the section that follows we unpack a set of vital practices that will support you as set out to establish your H3 habits so that you can live the Activated life. These will include learning about the Art of Letting Go and developing a conceptual understanding of the keys to Happiness. To help you develop a real-time understanding of when it is time to #GetActivated we will teach you how to listen to your body. You will discover the value of breathing practices and learn how to incorporate Movement and regular moments for meditation, prayer and contemplation.

Having said that I am under no illusion that this journey is an easy one, yet I have no doubt that every effort will be worth it. In fact, I am convinced that it helps you change your life as it has mine and many of my students and coaching delegates.

PART THREE

THE ART OF LETTING GO

Tao Te Ching
"When I let go of what I am, I become what I might be.
When I let go of what I have, I receive what I need".

FACING ADVERSITY

What do you typically find yourself doing in the face of adversity? Are you programmed to summon up all your strength, willpower, and courage or do you quickly succumb to your difficulties and retreat back into the safety of your comfort zone?

These are two normal and typical responses to seemingly overwhelming odds. Either you gather up the strength and courage to move forward or you give in to the moment under pressure. However, there is actually a third response. One that is more powerful and significantly more effective than the other two options. And that is to release and let go!

By "release and let go" I mean learning to surrender to the present moment. It means surrendering yourself to your current circumstances. Before you panic, allow me to me clarify. Surrendering is not the same as giving up. To give up means to quit taking action in the direction of your desired outcome. That is a form of retreat where you move away from something you desperately want and most likely actually need.

To surrender is like a "taking a momentary pause before taking another step" rather than making a full retreat. It gives you space to consider the environment as you make sense of the situation. It gives you space to process the circumstance and gather new insights and perspectives. It gives you space to create an opportunity from which you can move forward in a better way. It creates space to allow for positive change and nurture transformation.

When you practice surrender, you release all emotional attachment to past memories of failure and mistakes, to people who are holding you back, and to unhelpful thoughts and feelings that often sabotage your progress. When you release and let go, you're surrendering to the present moment. You're surrendering yourself to how things are right now and opening your heart and mind in a care-free state to new perspectives and the creation of opportunities.

This care-free state-of-mind doesn't only apply to moments when you are chasing your goals. It also applies to other circumstances when you face some kind of friction, unfamiliar change, problem, conflict or some form of discomfort.

Whenever you feel the need to fight and experience the struggle to resist, you aggravate your emotional state. When that happens, your vexed emotions cloud your judgment. They create a pattern of resistance where you struggle to see things clearly and objectively. As a result, you are more likely to make poor choices and get emotionally attached to the outcomes in the situation.

I need to be clear that in the practice of learning to release and let go; you are not trying to avoid the consequences of your challenging predicament. You're not forgetting what has happened or the reality of your circumstances. Rather, you are taking the time to clear your head so that you can gain a clearer perspective of the situation.

The art of learning to release and let go is all about taking responsibility for whatever situation you find yourself navigating. It is about stepping back and not allowing yourself to get overwhelmed by emotion that you experience in the moment. In learning to do this you allow space for positive change and transformation and develop the ability to respond more appropriately to the situation.

REASONS TO RELEASE AND LET GO!

Listen, don't get me wrong, I am not suggesting that learning to release and let go when facing difficulties is easy. There are however moments when it's beneficial to give yourself permission to step back, to release all attachment, and reassess your personal perspective of the situation.

For instance, learning to release and let go when you feel that your fears are getting the better of you. Release and let go when you find that you are consistently making unreasonable compromises. Release and let go when you recognize that you are have allowed yourself to sacrifice your personal values.

Learn to release and let go when you find that you are struggling to effectively deal with your hurts, regrets, failures, and mistakes. Release and let go when you find that you are holding a grudge against someone or deny yourself the opportunity for growth and personal development.

Learn to give yourself permission to disconnect from the weight of the emotional stress of all these things. They do not serve you. In the end they only serve to hurt you.

Holding onto these experiences as if they are your belongings will only weight you down. Holding on is in itself a learned practice that will only bring misery and despair into your life.

You do not have to invest so much of your energy resisting all the negative energy and experiences that life throws your way. The fact is the more you resist dealing with the negative stuff, the more it will pull you onto a roller coaster of endless regrets.

When you realize that you are holding onto too much negative thought it can feel like you have stepped into an emotional river of quicksand. Once you're knee deep in the muck, you feel kind of stuck. But look, this is only an illusion. You're not stuck. It only appears that way.

In the moment it sure doesn't feel that way so it is only natural that you resist. The problem is that more you resist facing the feelings the more it is like you struggle against the quicksand. Before you know it you are sinking deeper into the muck, you're way over your head and it feels like there is no way out. Again listen, it only feels that way.

Getting out of quicksand of emotion is about non-resistance. It's about stepping back from the drama and giving yourself time to think through your dilemma. It's about releasing and letting go of your struggles. Don't fight the quicksand. Instead, use it as a tool to help you get unstuck.

When you release and let go of 'fighting the situation' you free yourself to gain a creative perspective of the circumstance you find yourself in and free yourself to see things clearly. You can then use those insights to respond to the situation more appropriately and move forward in a better way.

KEYS TO HAPPINESS

The art of releasing and letting go is a vital key to learning to master the Heart Sense or emotional domain. A notable proportion of the struggles that you deal with as you learn to navigate the emotional domain are in fact self-inflicted. By that I mean they are ideas and beliefs that you have chosen to hold onto, regardless of whether they are valid or even true. These are the things that rob you of experiencing joy and happiness in your life.

What if I told you that it did not have to be this way? What if I told you that if you are willing to let go of certain things, that you can experience endless happiness. Would you believe me?

Listen, whether you are ready to believe me or not, how about you attempt an exercise?

In a moment I am going to invite you to consider a list of things that I would like you to release and let go. Yes, you heard me. It's a list of things that I want you to "just release" the need to care so deeply about.

Now I get it, some of these things are an important part of your life. But what if you just decided that these things didn't really matter as much as you have allowed them to? What if you decided that your happiness and emotional wellbeing is far more important? Would that not be worth a try?

Alright then, are you ready to give this a go? Here is a list of things that I invite you to release and let go of, starting today:

* Release and let go of past regrets.
* Release and let go of toxic friendships and relationships.
* Release and let go of taking criticism and rejection personally.
* Release and let go of agonizing over your mistakes.
* Release and let go of trying to be perfect.
* Release and let go of all doubts you have about your future and ability.
* Release and let go of all the things you can't change or control.

* Release and let go of everything you could potentially lose.
* Release and let go of all the fears that are holding you back from your dreams.
* Release and let go of attachment to specific results and outcomes.
* Release and let go of trying to live up to other people's standards or expectations of you.
* Release and let go of trying to win other people's approval.
* Release and let go of being dragged down by your feelings of guilt and shame.
* Release and let go of painful emotions that are keeping you stuck.
* Release and let go of your insecurities, unrealistic expectations and negative thoughts.
* Release and let go of being dragged down by other people's emotional outbursts and problems.
* Release and let go of holding onto choices you made, things that have failed or those you chose not to make.
* Release and let go of playing the victim of circumstance and instead start taking responsibility for creating a better life.

SIMPLE ENOUGH, RIGHT?

Well not exactly. Especially if this is the first time you are considering an exercise like this. Practicing the art of releasing and letting go of all these things will not be easy, however, it will definitely be worth it. Besides the acute and immediate emotional release, I want to assure you that you will be so grateful when it comes to your long-term happiness.

To start let me encourage you to try to release and let go of these things (or just a handful of them) for one day at a time.

After a few consecutive successful days try to release and let as many things on the list as possible, however now let's aim for an entire week. Then with more confidence and as you build momentum extend that week to a month and see how you go from there.

For now just start somewhere, anywhere. It will help to get the ball rolling. You might be wondering how to do this? How do we release and let go of all these things? There may even be a little voice scream from inside is it even really possible? The answer is a resounding YES even though it will take some planning and practice on your part.

> [Activation code] As you put this principle into practice you will learn to progressively focus on developing a few new habits and routines.

HOW TO RELEASE AND LET GO!

I can imagine you might want to say; 'but Robin, how do you actually implement this concept, like in the real world?'

Well, right up front let me tell you that there isn't one single answer. There isn't one miracle thing you can do that will immediately help you to release and let go of your emotional baggage. A better way to describe this journey is that as you put this principle into practice you will learn to progressively focus on developing a few new habits and routines. There are four phases to consider that will help you as you get started.

Phase 1: Recognize Moments of Attachment

The first phase to learn the art of release and let go is all about becoming aware. It's about recognizing moments when you start getting emotionally attached to things. During these moments you may feel a sense of discomfort or uncertainty. That's when you must recognize that it is time to release and let go.

Let's say that you feel like someone said something about or toward you that leaves you feeling criticized and you are struggling not to take it personally. Perhaps you reacted in a way that you immediately regretted and now find that you wish that you had not chosen to behave in that way.

Maybe you feel like you made a fatal mistake that you can't take back and now you find yourself feeling guilty about it. Or possibly you caught yourself doubting your own ability to achieve a goal. Whatever it may be for you, you will need to learn how to decide at that moment to release and let go.

To help you to release and let go during those critical moments, take the time to ask yourself the following set of questions:

- What idea or belief am I holding onto at that moment which triggers me to experience this particular emotion?
- How exactly does that make me feel?
- How does holding onto this feeling serve me in the short and/or long term?
- Why is that (which I am holding on to) so important for me?
- What value will I gain by letting go of this?
- What one simple thing can I do next to begin this process?

These questions are a great starting point. However, it's important that you don't stop there. You need to work through all four phases to fully release and let go.

Phase 2: Write Down Your Thoughts

The second phase of this process requires that you take the time to write down your thoughts on paper. This could look very much like your normal journaling exercise.

Take out a notebook or your journal and write down your thoughts and experiences for that day. Pay particular attention to capturing your concerns, problems, and all the things you struggled to release and let go. For perfectionist reader, I suggest a separate clean sheet of paper for this exercise.

Now give yourself permission to dig deep and list everything that made you experience a strain on your energy or emotion that particular day. Then having completed your list on the paper, take a deep breath, recognizing and acknowledging each individual aspect as you consciously decide to release and let all go of each one of these things.

A popular method that may help you develop a sense of closure in relation to the things on your list is to burn the page that you have written them on when you have finished the exercise. Yes, you heard me correctly. Actually rip the page out of your notebook, go outside and throw it into the fire or light the corner of the page and let it burn.

This symbolic ritual can become a powerful metaphor to help you to release and let go. And then, once it's done, just give yourself permission to move on. Leave the past in the past and choose to move forward with your life.

Now it might seem as such a simple thing however it can make a significant difference in the way you feel and think about your life and the choices you make.

Phase 3: Practice Becoming a Witness

The third phase may take some practice. It's all about creating an objective perspective and becoming a witness to your experience. This requires mentally stepping back from your problems and circumstances and viewing them from a third person's perspective. Picture yourself as an outsider looking on into the situation.

As a witness, you do not judge or criticize. You only contribute to your observation. You observe on both the outside and on the inside. In other words, you contribute what you observe about what's going on in the outside world, as well as what you are experiencing internally with your thoughts and feelings.

This is all about learning to become present and practicing mindfulness. It's about being truthful and honest about all your decisions, reactions and the emotions you experience, however with no self-judgment.

It's all about observation and self-reflection, which helps you to experience everything in a detached and objective manner. Done effectively this makes it much easier to release and let things go. It's easier because you are no longer emotionally engaged. Rather, you can process your list of things and the experience associated with each one in a rational and objective manner.

> [Activation code] Observation and self-reflection helps you to experience everything in a detached and objective manner. Living in the past will only hold you back in the present and prevent you from moving forward into your desired future.

Phase 4: Focus on Moving Forward, Not Backward

The final phase is to train yourself to focus on moving forward. If you're anything like I was then your life is also filled with many 'two steps forward, two steps back' experiences. We continuously move back and forth between our past, present, and future.

We desire to move forward into a favorable future, however, our regrets, mistakes, failures and all that other baggage pull us back into the past. Living in the past will hold you back in the present and prevent you from moving forward into your desired future.

It keeps you stuck and will hold you hostage. Moreover, it triggers and fuels into flame nasty emotions that make it very difficult to release and let go. When you're unable to release and let go you cannot move forward. This eats away at your sense of joy and happiness in the present moment.

One of the most productive ways to separate yourself from attachment you might experience to your past is to deliberately invest time in the practice of visualization. Regularly set aside to practice visualization. From my own experience I can recommend intentionally creating a time slot of at least 20 minutes the first few times that you put this practice into action.

Just visualize releasing and letting go of all the stuff that is weighing on your shoulders. With every breath, you release, visualize expelling these things out into the universe. And with every breath, you inhale visualize yourself drawing in positive energy that helps you to project more joy, compassion, and love into the world.

FOCUS ON THE PRESENT

Your ideal state-of-mind is to focus on the present. One of the best ways I have found to do this is through the practice of gratitude.

Take time to reflect on the things in your life that you can be grateful for. I like to use the head-heart-hand model to help me focus my thoughts. By that I mean consider what things come to my mind that I think of, that I feel or that I can physically experience that I can be grateful for.

When you are sitting down in a comfortable and conscious state ask yourself:
- What am I grateful for right now?
- Why do I appreciate having each of these things in my life?

The process of practicing gratitude will help bring your mind to the present. Then from there, you can focus on moving forward rather than backward.

USE A TOKEN AS A REMINDER TO LET GO!

One helpful method that you can use as a reminder to let go is to keep a token as a symbol in your pocket. This token can be a coin, marble, rock, or anything else that is relatively small. Alternatively, some people wear a ring on a finger, perhaps something on a necklace or chain that works in the same way.

Every time you touch or recognize this token, let it remind you to take a deep breath so that you can to release and let go of the weight you are carrying upon your shoulders at that moment. It's such a simple thing but it can make a significant difference to your experience of life.

TAKE TIME TO TALK WITH FAMILY AND FRIENDS

When you're struggling to let go of things you might find helpful to have a quick chat with family or close friends who you feel safe with.

Talk with them about your experiences, struggles, problems and the emotions you are going through. Ask them for their objective perspective on the matter. Listen to what they say. Perhaps they have some sage advice that can help you to release the emotional weight you are carrying upon your shoulders.

You might also find it helpful to ask these people the following questions:

- How have you previously managed to practice the art of learning to release let go?
- What tactics have worked best for you that might also work for me?
- What advice do you have that could help in my situation?

Keep in mind that other people might not have the answers you're searching for. However, their answers could very well provide insights that might help you find your answers somewhere else. Possibly even within your own self.

INCREASE YOUR MOBILITY

Another method that works extremely well to support your effort as you learn to release and let go comes in the form of movement and mobility or physical exercise.

When we're feeling stagnant and physically still, it can be challenging to release and let go. It's difficult because our physiology isn't in an ideal receptive or energized state. That changes very quickly when we're participating in regular physical exercise.

When you exercise, you are forced to move your body. This gets your heart pumping, stimulates hormone production, and as a result your entire physiology changes. Your brain finds it difficult to stay attached to all the stuff that has been weighing upon your shoulders. It's forced instead to focus on the present moment.

Physical exercise can allow you to feel like you are pressing the reset button on your brain. It reboots the system, and as a result, you experience more clarity of mind which helps you to think through situations more objectively and rationally.

Exercise also helps you make use of suppressed energy caught up in your body from unprocessed emotions. All the pent up energy can finally be released which then creates a physiological condition in which you can experience more clarity of mind.

There is no doubting the fact that we carry a lot of mental and emotional baggage around. Some of this baggage may seem rather small, insignificant and harmless. It is like walking around with a backpack that you choose to fill based on your life experiences. While you only have one brick of emotion the backpack might feel light and seem like it doesn't really matter. But you don't just carry one brick at a time, do you?

Nope, if you are anything like I used to be you choose to store a horde of bricks in that backpack, each stemming from a host of different things that you just can't seem to release and let go of. After some time this pack weighs heavily on your shoulders.

To release and let go you must start by removing one brick at a time. Yes, you might not feel any real difference at first, however, if you continue the process and keep removing just one brick at a time you will eventually feel the weight releasing from upon your shoulders.

That is when the burden of the world will no longer be yours, and you will have the freedom to experience true happiness and enjoy life to the fullest.

LEARNING TO LISTEN TO YOUR BODY

I can imagine that as you read this book you are developing a better sense of what you experience in your physical body. Today you might feel that you are more capable of articulating and making sense of those sensations than you have ever been before.

Over time, you will develop the ability to recognize when your body is telling you that something needs to change. It will become easier to discern when your body is opting for a sub-optimal state rather than choosing to act in a condition that can best support you become your most authentic version of yourself and achieve your ultimate performance.

> [Activation code] Your physical body is both the vehicle in which you experience your energetic state and the mechanism that has the most impact on the state of energy you experience.

You will become more sensitive of the state of energy that your body is engaged in. It's almost like driving your car and hearing that the motor is not engaged in the most appropriate gear. Sometimes it's not critical however it is clear that some of your operating systems are sub-optimal and you are working under unnecessary strain.

There are simple actions that you can take to intentionally shift the condition of your physical body into a state that better serves you. The key to remember as we unpack the following steps is that your physical body is both the vehicle in which you experience your energetic state and at the same time the mechanism that has the most immediate and direct impact on the state of energy you experience.

THERE IS LIFE IN MOVEMENT

One way to describe this is to ask you to become mindful of the sensation you experience in the current state of your physical body as you are reading this book. Without making any radical or intentional changes take a moment to become aware of how you are sitting.

Specifically, consider the way that you feel in your body as result of the posture of your back. Slowly become aware of the shape of your spine as you hold the book or device that you are reading from and how that influences your muscles all across your body.

Try to picture not only the large muscle groups in your lower and middle back but those also engaged in your arms and shoulders that are involved in holding up the book or mobile device in front of you as well. Now take a moment to examine how you feel in your physical body. And what is the impact of that physical feeling on how you experience your energy level right now?

The most acute manner to make a noticeable and immediate change to your body sense is to adjust the arch of your back or manipulate the shape of your spine. What if you did that right now? Slowly activate the muscles in your chest and shoulders and contract your stomach muscles as you bring your spine into a more upright position.

As you straighten your spine allow yourself to appreciate the change in the feeling or sensation across the muscles of your back, shoulders and neck. As you do this can you recognize a subtle but definite shift in the state of your energy you experience? Can you feel that somehow the energy that you experience in your body has 'lifted'?

Perhaps a moment ago you felt stagnant or dull as if the energy resonating through your body was vibrating at very low or poorly charged levels. One could say that your energy was unable to get into the flow as it was compressed by the physical state of your body. As soon as you chose to change the stance of your body you created a shift in your physical experience that allowed for a shift in your emotional and then energetic experience.

You have in effect made the conscious decision to change your energetic state through an intentional decision to make a change to your physical body.

THERE IS LIFE IN THE MUSIC

The same can be achieved through music. Do you remember my experience at the local CrossFit gym that I mentioned at the opening of this book? I described the influence of the music selection on my ability to engage in the exercise. This is actually one of the most helpful tactics that I have used to help me complete the manuscript of this book.

In fact, it is the most effective tactic I have found that I can use whenever I need to engage in deep work. I consciously play music in the background, whether in my office or through headphones to change the energetic state that I experience when I sit down to write.

I even have a particular folder on my desktop called "Choose my State" with a selection of music tracks that I have saved. This is a selection of songs, mostly instrumental yet in various genre and styles that I play as background music while I work. It's often quite a magical experience. I feel my energy state shift, my focus is steady and my ability to concentrate for longer periods of time improves.

THERE IS LIFE IN THE LIGHT

Another simple action that you can take to intentionally shift the condition of your physical body into a more positive state is to consider your access to light and oxygen.

Have you ever noticed how the amount of natural light you are exposed to can have a significant impact on the way that you feel? Consider for a moment your regular working station. If that is in an office environment take a moment to a look around and notice how much natural light are you normally exposed to?

Now imagine with me for a moment you are sitting in one of your favorite spots where you feel you can be creative and productive. How different is that environment, how much natural light are you exposed to and how much fresh air do you have access to?

Think back to our conversation earlier in the book about the insight you can learn from your eyesight. Another way you can have a relatively immediate impact on the state you experience in your physical body is to adjust the amount of natural light that you are exposed to. If you have a window in the room that you are in make sure that it is open and that the curtains are drawn open to let the light in. If you do not have access to a window to allow natural light in make sure that you have a bright enough light source in the room that you are sitting in.

You can engage this ability to create a state shift in your physical body as soon as you wake up and allow as much light in your room as possible. This will create a positive shift in your energy right at the start of your day. Even better how about getting outside as soon as possible first thing in the morning and maximizing your direct exposure to sunlight? While you are out there, it's also the best time to increase the amount of oxygen that you get into your system.

THERE IS LIFE IN THE BREATH.

One of the most effective ways to shift the condition of your physical body into a more positive state and one that has a noticeable and immediate impact is that of active or intentional breathing.

This is far more than the natural or instinctive shallow breathe that you are probably familiar to. The truth is that most people have lost the ability to breathe in a way that best serves their body. It is like they have become lazy breathers. Let me ask you if you were to become more aware of your breathing right now as you read this, how would you describe it? By that I mean how would you describe how much oxygen air is getting into your body through the air you take in?

The fact that I am drawing attention to it probably means that your body has already started taking in a slightly deeper breathe. Only a moment ago you were breathing pretty much only in your throat, perhaps the very top of your lungs. If you were an observer sitting in the room watching you, you might notice that your shoulders hardly moved.

In this modern age of instant porridge and microwave popcorn I fear some of us have forgotten how to breathe. I don't mean the shallow gasp of polluted air we rely on as we rush about or day. I mean the deep inhale of life-giving breath, like you would if you were standing on the edge of a cliff high up in the mountains and you can taste the cool fresh air as you fill your chest with breath.

YOUR BRAIN NEEDS OXYGEN

Your brain needs oxygen to function at its best. It needs oxygenated blood to flow through it so that it can perform to its intended potential. But most of us have become familiar with a weak life of shallow breathing.

When last did you enjoy the experience of fully oxygenated blood flowing through your body? I don't mean with the help of some external medical implement. I mean through using your god given breathing apparatus to the full extent of their capacity.

TRY THIS SIMPLE EXERCISE

Find a quiet stress free environment where you can sit comfortably, with you back shaped with good posture and your feet placed firmly on the floor so as to ground you.

For a moment, as you breathe in and out in a normal easy pattern, allow your mind to settle down by focusing your attention on the rise and fall of your chest. You will begin to notice your breath. You will begin to notice the rhythm and pace as you take a breath in and release the air out.

Relaxing the muscles in your shoulders, and your neck, you will feel that you can begin to take a slightly deeper breathe. Until now you might only have been using your throat and perhaps only the very top of our lungs to breathe. If you think about it, this is only a portion of your breathing capacity that your body is relying on to oxygenate your blood supply and feed the rest of your body.

Work in sets of three deep intakes. Increase the volume of air that you take in with each breath while still keeping a steady and even rhythm. Do this for four cycles of three intakes, increasing the volume of air you take into your body with each cycle.

I encourage you to give this a try. It's quite a rush when you feel your brain almost pulsating with so much oxygen flowing through it. You will feel like you are on a high. You may feel a little light-headed the first time that you do this, especially if you have been in the practice of shallow breathing for some time.

It is important to note that taking up a new practice such as this for the first time should be done with caution. It is advisable to consult your medical professional for expert advice about a practice that is best suited for your body in the condition or state of health that you are in.

THERE IS LIFE IN YOUR BELLY

The next simple exercise, the belly breath, will help you develop better control of your breathing. Begin activating your breath by pushing out your belly. As you do this, you will pull air in through your nostrils deep into your lungs.

Then activate your belly, pulling it all the way in as if you can touch your spine with your stomach muscles. As you do this you're pushing all the air from your lungs out through the nostrils.

The next level of the belly breath is to activate the diaphragm after you have used your belly. In practice, your belly will fill with air and then, as if it is a second stage, your chest will lift as you activate your diaphragm to fill your body cavity with even more air.

The exhale is the same, activating the diaphragm and then the belly as you push out all the air in your lung and chest cavity.

A third level of this exercise is to activate the chest after you have engaged the belly and diaphragm, increasing the size of your body cavity as you fill your lungs even further.

AN ENERGETIC OXYGEN BOOST

Here is an exercise for the more advanced reader. If you are someone who has developed your breath work and are physically healthy and consider yourself to be fit. When done correctly you will feel more vitalized and alert than you might have in a very long time.

Sit in an upright yet comfortable position with your feet ground firmly on the floor and your eyes closed. In this exercise you will be rapidly increasing the volume of air that you take in using your upper body and arms. There are three steps.

With your back straight, reach up into the sky with your hands fully extended as if to touch the sky. As your arms extend up fill your lungs to full capacity with a deep breath. Inhale through your nose and take the air into your gut, as deep as you can.

Next you will pull down your arms quickly, with your elbows tucked in along the side of your body, closing your hands into a fist as you do this. Exhale as much air as you can as your hands drop to your chest, pushing out every last drop of breath. This is a quick and vigorous movement. Start gently at first so that you do not to hurt your back and shoulders.

Now shoot you arms back above your head and inhale a deep breath as your hands reach up into the sky, filling up as much of your chest as possible. You can visualize filling your entire upper body cavity with air as you inhale through your nose.

Repeat this movement, arms explode up and inhale – arms drop down and exhale, for a repetition of 30 counts. Then with your eyes remaining closed and your feet grounded on the floor, allow your hands to drop onto your lap with your palms facing up. Remain in this rest position for a count of twenty or about 10 seconds.

To get the best out of this energetic oxygen boost you can start with three rounds of 30 reps (counts), then 20 reps and finally 10 reps, making sure to take a rest in between each cycle.

This is a great opportunity to develop your ability to become body conscious. In the rest between each cycle bring your attention on the sensation you will experience in your physical body. You might feel the rapid increase of your heartbeat and the rush of blood flowing through your body. You may also feel a slight tingling, particularly in your extremities like your fingers, as now oxygen-rich blood flows through your body. If this is the first time you have done an activity of this nature in a while, you will feel a little ligh-headed and perhaps even a little dizzy.

Now is a great time to set aside five to ten minutes for meditative breathing when you have completed the three cycles of the energetic oxygen boosted breathing. For the experienced reader I recommend a cycle of square breathing.

SQUARE OR BOX BREATHING

What is square or box breathing you might ask? This is another great active or tactical breathing technique that takes the belly breath technique a step further.

Just like in the belly breathe exercise find a quiet stress free environment. Sit comfortably, with your back in a good posture and your feet placed firmly on the floor so as to ground you.

Begin to breathe in and out in a normal easy pattern, allow your mind to settle down by focusing your attention on the rise and fall of your chest. Activate your chest, diaphragm and belly as you take in three deep breaths, releasing them in a slow and controlled manner.

Now for the square or box part, starting with a count of three. Take a deep activated breath in, making sure to breathe in slowly for a count of three. By that I mean take a full three seconds to fill your lungs. This is the first side of the square or box.

At the top of the cycle, with your chest activated and lungs filled, hold that breathe in for a count of three. This is the second side of the box.

Begin to slowly release the breath making sure to use the same activation as in the belly breath. The idea is to release the air from your lungs in a way that it takes a full three counts before all the air is exhaled. This is the third side of the box.

Finally, when you are at the bottom of the cycle, with your lungs now empty of breathe, hold that compression on your chest for a count of three. This 'empty breathe' is the fourth side of the box.

You are now ready to repeat the square or box breathing cycle. This kind of breathing is often referred to as tactical breathing as it is the technique used by soldiers and highly trained special forces to intentionally create calm and maintain focus of their executive functions under extreme pressure.

For the advanced reader you can explore more complex versions of square breathing where you increase the time or count of each 'side' as you develop your lung capacity. Please be careful if you are only starting out with these exercises if you rush it you can easily faint or pass out losing consciousness for a moment and possibly even injure yourself. Practice caution, especially as you begin.

THERE IS LIFE IN MEDITATION

The practice of meditation is known by many names, largely depending on the culture or belief system that you are a part of. In my understanding there are a few things happening on the three levels.

Whether you choose to attach more spiritual or cultural significance on any one of these is up to you. Even if you know the practice by another name, the outcome is still the same. Do not get stuck in how you describe or what you are familiar to call it and miss the magic of what the practice will unlock for you in your life.

In the simplest form meditation is the physical practice of calming your mind and releasing trapped emotional energy. Just from the perspective of your energetic state this experience can be quite a spiritual encounter.

HERE ARE A FEW GUIDELINES MEDITATION.

The practice of meditation will require that you can focus your mind. To do that, you will need to place yourself in an environment that you have some control or influence over.

You will want to be able to manage the light and sound. Too bright and you will suffer over stimulation. Vice versa too dark and you will probably only fall asleep. Too noisy and you will find it very difficult to manage your thoughts as you focus your mind. Yet too quiet and you might either fall asleep or the noise of the quiet can feel deafening.

You will also want to have influence over a few physical elements like the temperature and the level of physical comfort you experience. Too hot and you will struggle to focus your mind wanders and eventually becomes sluggish while your body tries to cool down and self regulate. Too cold and your body will steal all your attention to that of ensuring survival as you begin to shiver in an attempt to raise your core body temperature.

The most effective way that I have learned to engage in the practice of meditation is to implement what I learned in belly breathing. Are you ready to give this a go?

Make sure that you are sitting comfortably with good posture and your feet placed firmly on the ground. If at all possible I would encourage you to find a spot where you can take your shoes off and settle feet on the grass so that your body can be grounded to the earth.

In a normal easy pattern, begin to breathe in and out focusing your attention on the rise and fall of your chest. As you breathe become aware of your natural rhythm, allowing your energy to resonate in a positive 'vibration'.

With your hands resting on your lap, palms open and facing upwards, continue to breathe deeply. As you allow a sense of peace to grow allow your mind to think of a safe place, a memory that you feel grateful for or a moment that you felt at your best.

As you experience that positive state begin to ask that anything that needs healing in your body be healed. Breathe as you would if you felt a warm white light of healing poured into every part of your physical body. Light that slowly saturates all your organs. Passing through your blood and bringing healing as it goes. Light so gentle yet so strong that it seeps deep into your bones.

Then imagine with me an energy that comes from above through the top of your head, perhaps something of a pearl of blue light, and as you take a breath in, let the air of energy go down into your body. Imagine the blue pearl of energy light go down into you, through your chest and into the stomach. See the energy swirl down to your legs, through your claves and into your feet before dropping deep into the earth.

Imagine the pearl of energy circulating the earth before it comes back up from the deep into your feet. Feel it swirling through your legs, your calves and into your stomach, rising slowly up into your chest. See the blue light bringing healing with it as it moves through to the top your head and high up into the heavens.

See the vortex of blue energy coming down through the top of your head, swirling through your chest down into your legs. Feel the energy pass through your feet reaching into the deep and circulating the earth before coming back up. Feel the energy surge through your feet, swirling up through your legs and into your chest.

See the vortex of blue energy as light swirling through your body, and as it does, it brings healing and love wherever it goes. Now then for the next few minutes allow your mind to find focus on your intentions for the day.

When you are ready slowly start to move or wiggle your fingers allowing the energy stored up in your body to move through your hands. You might want to gently shake your hands as you slowly open your eyes again. When you are fully alert again take three sharp deep belly breaths before you get up and continue with your day.

MEDITATION WITH A GUIDE

Well I hope that you had the courage to give that a try. If you are familiar with the practice of meditation, I hope you were inspired to revisit it and give it another go. I can tell you this has been one of the most valuable practices that I have learned to include in my life, one I now implement daily.

Oh, and one more thing, if you are anything like me and have what can be described as a concrete or sequential thinking style. Or if you consider yourself to be predominantly a logical thinker and you are really struggling with the idea of a blue pearl of energy and how it can just magically come through the top of your head, here is an idea that I have found very helpful.

When you are at that moment in your meditation where you want to allow the energy to come into your experience, I find it helpful to think from the perspective God as he looks down on me. I imagine I am with him, as if we are a thousand feet directly above me. Then I imagine in my mind's eye that pearl of light falling, closer and closer until it penetrates the top of my head and deep into my physical body as a vortex of energy. I find this allows me to receive the experience and make it my own.

If perhaps you find it a little of a struggle to do this by yourself, you may find it useful to apply a mental aid. Something like a mantra can support you keep your focus and maintain your concentration as you develop your ability to practice meditation. A mantra is not some kind of witchcraft or voodoo. It is simply a chosen word or phrase that makes up a sound which is repeated in a rhythmical manner to aid concentration in meditation.

It does not have to be complicated. Actually, I find that the simplest word or phrase is often the more effective. The key is to slowly repeat the word or phrase in a rhythm that supports deep belly breath and allows your mind to become focused and clear.

Here are a few ideas to start with. Quite often people begin to use meditation when they feel the need to deal with anxiety or stress. A great mantra to use in this situation is "release".

Another word that I have used in a time when I want to use the practice of meditation to allow for healing is the word "restore'. A phrase that I have often used for motivation and self-care is the phrase "I am enough". The mantra that I often use to build myself up in times of uncertainty or as a refreshing way to start the day is "I am wonderfully made".

So how does using a mantra actually work you may ask. It is really as simple as it sounds. You can use the same approach as we described for the belly breath or simple square breathing. Sitting comfortably with your back in a good position and your feet grounded, begin to take a deep breath. Then at the top of the cycle, just before you begin to exhale, you insert or use your mantra.

Let's say, for example, that you want to use the "release' mantra to meditate as you aim to release and let go of anxiety. In your activated breathing position, take a deep breath in. As you begin to exhale use the first part of your stored breath to say the word "release'.

Activating your chest, diaphragm and belly force the rest of the air out of your lungs. Then activating your belly, diaphragm and chest to inhale fill your lungs, holding the air for a moment before saying the word "release" as you exhale. You can repeat this as long as you are comfortable to continue the self-guided meditation practice.

You may well find that your mind wants to wonder from thought to thought as the trapped energy is slowly released. When you have stopped using the mantra and want to regain focus again to continue, simply start the phrase again at the top of the next breath cycle.

When you feel that you have sufficiently completed the meditation practice slowly start to wiggle your fingers. This allows the energy stored up in your body to move through to your hands. You may feel like you want to gently shake your hands as you slowly open your eyes again and return to a conscious alert state. Take three quick deep belly breaths and you will be ready to continue with what you were busy with.

Another form of guided meditation is to use a verbal or vocal guide. There are a number of really helpful apps and online resources where you can download or purchase a meditation which has been prepared with both a music track in the background as well as a person talking you through a structured practice.

Much like how I have explained each of the breathing and meditation practices, a person will narrate a particular meditation in a way that you can follow along. I find that these are very helpful particularly when working into an unfamiliar aspect or to expand my meditation 'vocabulary'.

When using a guided meditation the same principles apply to the breathing and simple meditation exercises that we have discussed however I would strongly encourage you to consider using headphones so that you can get the most out of the practice.

THAT ALL THINGS CAN BE RENEWED

This next section is a topic that many people may not have heard much about before that is energy medicine and the emotion code. I heard about the principles a few years back but back was not ready to embrace concepts like quantum physics, neurobiology or ancient healing. At that time so it sounded too 'out there' for my confidence and understanding.

Fast forward a few years and today I find myself completely into the 'out there' stuff because of the incredible effects it has had on me and so many of the people who I work with. One particular aspect of energy medicine that fits so well with our current conversation is that of the Emotion and Body Code.

ENERGY MEDICINE

Looking for a Left Brain Definition:

> "Conventional medicine, at its foundation, focuses on the biochemistry of cells, tissue, and organs. Energy Medicine, at its foundation, focuses on the energy fields of the body that organize and control the growth and repair of cells, tissue, and organs. Changing impaired energy patterns may be the most efficient, least invasive way to improve the vitality of organs, cells, and psyche."
>
> – David Feinstein, Ph.D

Perhaps a Right Brain Definition:

"Energy is your body's magic! It is your life force. You keep it healthy and it keeps you healthy. If you are sick or sad, shifting your energies feels good. When you care for these invisible energies, it makes your heart sing and your cells happy!"

– Donna Eden

When talking about conventional medicine we are really describing functional and traditional forms of medicine as a means to deal with and treat the physical body. The shortcoming of this perspective is that the physical body not only a 'physical' system. It is a complex and dynamic system that is influenced and controlled by the networks of energy that run through it.

I believe that we are designed to have a flow of constant life energy that is supposed to be flowing through our bodies to keep us in physical, mental and emotional state of health. When that energy is not flowing correctly we recognize and diagnose problems as they begin to manifest in our physical body. Much of conventional medicine is designed from the attempt to treat these diagnoses rather than understand or treat the source.

"If you want to find the secrets of the universe, think in terms of energy, frequency and vibration.
- Nikola Tesla

"Everything in life is vibration."
- Albert Einstein

EVERYTHING IS ENERGY

Every person, place, and object is made up of energy. That energy can be described as particles resonating at a particular frequency or vibration. Different things are vibrating at different levels and a unique frequency.

If you are feeling love, joy, thankfulness, peace you are experiencing the energy of that emotion. Each emotional experience is the physiological sensation of that energy at a particular frequency. When you experience these positive emotions, you are vibrating at a high frequency or level. When a body of matter is resonating at a particular frequency, it will seem to be drawn to other bodies that are in that same vibration.

In the same way if you are feeling anger, worry, jealousy you are experiencing a physiological sensation of the energy of that emotion. You are vibrating at what is described as a very low level. At this level you will seem to draw other low vibration people and situations into your environment. This is why it is so vital to become consciously aware of what you are thinking and feeling in any given moment.

EMOTIONS ARE ENERGY AND IMPACT THE BODY

What if trapped emotions, anxieties, and unprocessed life experiences that we hold in our nervous system are a main source of everything that lead our body to manifest disease?

Emotion is a form of energy that you experience in a physiological sensation. If so, then each one could be measured and calibrated. When you experience a traumatic or intense emotion, the energy of that emotion can literally get stuck inside the body. When low vibration energy is stuck in the human body, it allows for a condition where imbalances, disease, pain, mental, physical and emotional problems begin to manifest or materialize.

The low vibration stuck in the body then attracts other bodies of low vibration like that of parasites, bacteria and viruses. This in turn can act to weaken your immune system. If this is the case many symptoms of a body in dis-ease, manifesting complex problems like the discomfort of back pain, the frustration of rhinitis, to darkness of depression and angst of anxiety, even the onset of cancer, or something as simple as acne and anything in between could be caused by destructive impact of low vibration energy of a trapped emotion.

Say you struggle with anxiety. If you have a trapped emotion of anxiety stuck in your body, then technically 'anxiety' is always there so you get easily triggered by any little situation that could bring it on. I have read researchers who claim that as much as 95% of disease and imbalances are caused by our emotional thought life!

Dr. Bradly Nelson, author of the emotion code noticed through his clinical practice that almost every person that came to see him had stuck emotions that were at the root of their problem.

TRAPPED EMOTIONS

Dr Nelson suggests that trapped emotions can happen in two ways:

1. The emotion that you experience from a certain stimulus, be that a situation, environment or event.

2. An inherited emotion. There is evidence to suggest that negative emotions can get passed down through the generations.

A HEART OF WALLS

Dr Nelson also mentions how the greatest discovery in energy medicine is the heart wall. What is the heart wall?

Over the years (and while we are in the womb) we go through many different traumatic and emotional events in life. In some of these experiences, you can actually physically feel your heartache.

When this happens, he suggests that your heart forms a layer of energy over it in an effort to protect you. Over the years, you can have layers and layers of trapped emotions that form what is called a heart wall.

How can you tell if you have developed a heart wall:

1. Low energy, low immune system.
2. Indecisiveness (what is my mission in life).
3. Desensitized heart (difficulty to give/receive love).

4. Poor communication – when two people have heart walls, they can experience communication issues, often getting triggered but without knowing why.

5. Abundance and wealth issues.

Clearing your heart wall is like clearing all of your emotional clutter from your life that you have allowed to accumulate over the years. Emotions and beliefs that cause you to be easily triggered and react in certain ways, see the world from a certain perspective and interact with people in ways that you do not understand do not serve your purpose.

The amount of sessions it takes to clear your heart wall is different for everyone because different people may have more or less trapped emotions depending on their past.

FINDING AND TRAPPED ENERGY

The process of the emotion code is simple and makes uses of applied kinesiology or muscle testing. Muscle testing is said to be a helpful tool however it is worth noting that is best to work with someone who has proven experience to get an accurate and meaningful result.

Consider that your brain can process about 400 billion bits of information per second. It is said that the conscious mind can process about 40 to 200 bits per second of data while your subconscious mind can process in the region of 20 000 000 bits per second. That means the subconscious mind can process data 500 000 times more efficiently than the conscious mind. Consider that conscious mind runs your autonomic body. It keeps you heart eating while you don't have to think about it, it makes sure that you put out your left foot after your right as you take your next step.

Simple acts of walking, breathing or even blinking are all highly complex functions all managed by the sub-conscious mind. In a similar way your sub-conscious mind is also processing complex emotional and energetic interactions in your environment around you, the majority of which are not visible to your conscious mind or the naked eye.

Muscle testing can be described as a gross motor or physiological reflection of what is happening in your sub-conscious mind. There are a few simple steps to conduct a muscle test.

Step 1. Muscle test to see if they are testable by asking a 'neutral' or 'confirmation' question. The simplest form of this is to ask them to say their name, conduct the test, and the response should be strong. Then, ask them to say that their name is "Batman" or something that is not their name and the muscle test response should be weak.

There are a few relatively simple ways that you can conduct the muscle test. The most well known is to observe the subjects arm, held out extended either to their side or in front of them. The actual test is to observe the variation or fluctuation of the strength of the muscle behavior in response to the test question, hence the application of kinesiology.

Holding your hand above their arm and applying a slight but consistent amount of pressure, you will notice a steady demonstration of strength or amount of resistance in their arm in response to the 'positive' or 'true' question. By that I mean in a truthful response the subject will be able to hold their arm up steadily with little effort or struggle.

When processing a question expected to be false you will observe the subject demonstrate quite a different response. Their ability to maintain a steady resistance to the pressure you are applying on their arm will change dramatically. In effect it will seem as if the subject loses strength in their arm as it easily gives way to your pressure. In this case it will be considered as a physiological reflection that the answer to your question is false.

Step 2. Before each session, it is important to pause and ask for God's help. I like to think of this as inviting the light in to provide guidance and accuracy. Dr Nelson suggests that the greatest job of a healer is to act as the go-between because it is God that is revealing and leading the session and you and I are just the ones he uses.

Step 3. Next, ask a 'test' question. For example, " is there a trapped emotion causing this ___ (pain, anxiety, anger, disease, etc). The questions you can ask are endless!

Step 4. You look at the descriptions below and ask:

a). Is it in column A, Is it in column B

    b). Having identified the column you can now ask which row is it in namely 1,3,5 or 2,4,6.

c). Having identified the row you can go through each emotion in that particular row.

d). When you identify an emotion, simply take a magnet or your hand and run it over the governing meridian holding the intention of clearing that emotion.

e). Ask the subject if the emotion is cleared. You can use further muscle testing to confirm this.

The description below describe the contents of a table from The Emotion Code chart (c) 2007-2016 Wellness Unmasked In. The row indicates the location of emotion or energy trapped in the body, and where column A or column B indicates the symptom or manifestation of the emotion experienced.

ROW = location of trapped energy or emotion	
Column A = manifestation or symptom	Column B = manifestation or symptom
Row 1. Heart or small intestine	
Abandonment, Betrayal, Forlon, Lost, Love unreceived.	Effort unreceived, Heartache, Insecurity, Overjoy, Vulnerability
Row 2. Spleen or stomach	
Anxiety, Dispair, Disgust, Nervousness, Worry	Failure, Helplessness, Lack of Control, Low Self-esteem
Row 3. Lung or colon	
Crying, Discouragement, Rejection, Sadness, Sorrow	Confusion, Defensiveness, Grief, Self-Abuse, Stubbornness
Row 4. Liver or Gall Bladder	
Anger, Bitterness, Guilt, Hatred, Resentment.	Depression. Frustration, Indecisiveness, Panic, Taken for Granted
Row 5. Kidneys or Bladder	
Blaming, Dread, Fear, Horror, Perceived Conflict	Creative Insecurity, Terror, Unsupported, Wishy washy
Row 6. Glands and Sexual Organs	
Humiliation, Jealousy, Longing, Lust, Overwhelm	Pride, Shame, Shock, Unworthy, Worthlessness

Often times, an issue you are dealing with will like a physical pain can dramatically decrease or even instantly disappear. Sometimes it can take a few sessions for a thorough clearing of the heart wall to be successful.

Even if you don't feel anything at first, clearing the negative energy of low frequency out of your body allows all organs and physiological systems to work more optimally. In the weeks that follow you may find that you are less easily emotionally triggered.

KEEP AN OPEN MIND

If all if this sounds a little weird for you, trust me, I totally get you. When I first encountered this body of knowledge I was completed closed to it. All my social and cultural conditioning told me that this way of thinking was taboo. So I just wrote it off at first. Over time, I have come to understand that's just because it's a different and unfamiliar yet ancient way of thinking.

If you have tried just about everything to heal like working with your diet, taking supplements, improving your sleep, even taking specialized medicines and are still having mental and physical issues, perhaps it's time to consider some form of energy medicine.

CONCLUSION

The truth is that you don't have to do anything about what we have discussed here so far. To be honest, it would actually make sense to me if you don't. I understand if you choose to rather leave things the way that they were. I mean, for sure that would be the easier option.

Choosing to live the Activated life will not be easy and there is no magic pill to make these changes happen overnight. But what will that cost you?

As of this moment you have in your hands a framework that shows you how to actively consider your reaction in any situation you find yourself in. You have access to a set of tactics that will help you identify the stimuli that trigger you most. This means you no longer have to be trapped by a reaction that for some unknown reason seems to have a pull on you.

As you develop your Activated H3 habits, you will be empowered to see the beliefs that you have bought into which no longer serve you. You will be able to recognize a behaviour response that you might have previously opted for before you set about self-sabotaging your dreams and goals.

As you put the Activated Intelligence Trifecta into practice, you will learn to sharpen your intuition and have a clear understanding of what you value most and why that is important to you. This will give you a real-time insight as you engage cognitive arousal and apply rational thought to processing the facts of the situation you find yourself in.

Armed with these insights you will be able to develop what can seem like an unfair advantage in any situation as you learn to actively regulate your emotional reactions. That means that you can consciously select an intentional H3 behavior response and as you do this more often learn how to reinforce your desired behavior across the H3 triad.

This will mean that you are able to process your feelings (emotions), consider your thoughts (thinking), get in touch with your physiological (sensation) response and unpack your emotion-related behavior (actions) so that you can unlock the power to be able to shift from an instinctive reaction and select an intentional response.

Now you are ready to live the Activated Life!

ABOUT THE AUTHOR

Inspiring and infectious, Robin Pullen has a warm dynamic presence that fills the room. He is a masterful speaker who is able to connect across a multitude of cultures, meeting each individual at their level. He leaves the listener inspired to be more and motivated to take massive action.

Yet Robin does not leave you there, he has developed the competence to empower people for change. Armed with the insights, technology and tactics that he has crafted through training more than 100'000 people in the first five years of his professional career, Robin is on a mission to activate 10 million people in the next ten years to action so that they can achieve more than they had imagined possible through personal, professional and business mastery.

Robin Pullen is actively engaged in his mission to empower 10 million people over the next ten years so that they can discover that everything they need for success and significance already lies within their reach.

At 15 he suffered a boating accident on the foreshore of Hartbeespoort Dam in the foothills of the Magaliesberg mountain range. Suffering a severe injury with a laceration right through his calf muscle that very nearly reached the bone the attending doctor told him he would not be able to run normally again.

Just over two years later he was back on his feet and competing in the prestigious Premier Hockey League, playing for his High School Old Boys Club (PHOBIANS) men's senior side, while still a standard nine (grade eleven) scholar at school.

"I can still remember the look on his face when I literally bumped into my physiotherapist on the basketball court at the campus. At first all he could do was stare. Then after what felt like a few minutes, he said it was like looking at a ghost. That I shouldn't be able to run like this, never mind be playing such an aggressive sport out there on the outdoor court."

At 30 he co-founded his first company and was told his training and development methods could not be done, and that the business model would never work.

Robin Pullen is considered a thought leader and behavior management expert who practices as a professional speaker and has worked with more than 100'000 people, all before he turned 40. As a trusted business advisor and executive business coach his clients have taken him with them into 9 countries across the African continent. His learning materials and training products have been translated into 13 languages including French, Malagasy, Mandarin and Swahili.

Index

A

abstract, 40
Acknowledge, 125
actions, 48
Activated intelligence, 99
activation, 51
active attention, 41
adjustment, 66
Adrenaline, 53
adrenals, 55
adversity, 136
aesthetic, 60
affirmations, 132
aggressive, 37
alertness, 41, 51
amygdala, 35
analytical, 64
Anger, 65
anosognosia, 50
antecedent, 67
Antidepressants, 80
anxiety, 54
Anxiety, 65, 79
Appraisal, 66
Arousal, 51
attended stimulus, 45
attention, 51
Attention, 66
Attention deployment, 68
authenticity, 104
autonomic nervous system, 30
awareness, 41, 44

B

balance, 27
basal ganglia, 37
behavior, 14, 120
beliefs, 48, 57, 118, 120
belonging, 59
beta blockers, 73
biologically, 50
body conscious, 89
brain, 24
brainwaves, 50
break free, 106
breathing, 90
brightness, 43

C

caffeine, 134
caliber, 92
calories, 93
cardiovascular, 53
care-free, 137
Cartesian, 48
categories, 46
categorize, 46
cellular, 38
cerebellum, 27
cerebral cortex, 27, 30
cerebrum, 31

change, 107
chemicals, 51
choice, 127
circumstance, 125
Classical conditioning, 58
cognition, 40
Cognitive Appraisal Theory, 76
cognitive arousal, 108, 121
cognitive awareness, 63
Cognitive change, 70
combativeness, 37
compassion, 62
comprehension, 31
conceptual, 40
concrete, 40
conscious, 40
Consciousness, 47
contemplation, 133
Contempt, 65
context, 42
control, 66
conventional medicine, 103
conviction, 104, 107
cornea, 41
corpus callosum, 31
Cortisol, 55
courage, 93
culture, 107
curiosity, 108

D

deliberate, 121
demonstrate, 122
Depression, 65
Descartes, 48
desensitized, 88
dictated, 126
diencephalon, 28
Disgust, 65
displeasure, 37
Distancing, 72
distracted, 93
Distraction, 69
disturbance, 123
domains, 99
Dopamine, 52
dopaminergic, 35
Dorsal, 28
Drug use, 73
dualistic, 47

E

electrical impulses, 19
electromagnetic, 41
emotion related responses, 29
Emotional, 34
Emotional Intelligence, 62
emotional reactivity, 36
emotional related responses, 121
emotional state, 89, 98
emotionally, 99
empathize, 62
Empathy, 62
empowered, 119
endorphins, 53
energy, 19

Envy, 65
epinephrine, 53
esteem, 59
Execute, 125
executive functions, 50
Executive functions, 32
Exercise, 73
expressions, 64
Expressive suppression, 72

F

fatigue, 117
Fear, 65
feelings, 64
fight or flight, 53
filter, 118
fitness, 134
flow, 109
forebrain, 26
frontal lobe, 32

H

habit, 107
Hand sense, 101
happiness, 91
Happiness, 65
Head Sense, 101
Heart sense, 100
hemispheres, 31
hesitating, 94
Higher brain, 50
hijacked, 92

hippocampus, 36
homeostasis, 83
Homeostasis, 86
hormones, 51
HPA axis, 80
hue, 43
humor, 53
Humor, 72
hunger, 37
hypothalamus, 29, 36

I

Identify, 125
immune system, 83
incantations, 132
inconsistency, 105
inhibiting, 63
initiating, 63
injury, 39
insulin, 55
Integrate, 125
intellectually, 99
intention, 44, 132
intentional, 98
intentional response, 15
interpret, 46
intestine, 53
intrinsic, 64
intuitive, 40

J

John Locke, 49

K

Karl Marx, 49
kinesthesia, 21
***Knowledge needs**, 61*

L

language, 31
laughter, 37
learned skill, 92
lens, 42
leveraging, 120
limbic system, 34

'Locus of Control, 16

L

logical reasoning, 31
Love, 65
lung, 90

M

mammalian, 30
manipulate, 106
Maslow's Hierarchy of needs, 58
materialism, 49
meaning, 42
meditation, 133
medulla oblongata, 26, 30
memory, 42

mental model, 117
mental models, 132
mental processes, 24
mental state, 89
mental states, 48
metabolism, 36
midbrain, 25
mind-body problem, 48
modulating, 64
Moral needs, 61
motivate, 75
motivation, 75
Mumford's needs, 60
muscle contraction, 53
muscle coordination, 27

N

nerve impulses, 52
neural impulses, 22, 42
neurons, 22
Neurons, 52
neuroplasticity, 32
Neuroplasticity, 38
neurotransmission, 52
neurotransmitter, 52
Neurotransmitters, 52
Neutral, 65
noradrenaline, 54
noradrenline, 53
Norepinephrine, 54
Nummenmaa, 64

O

obstruction, 123
occipital lobe, 33
operant conditioning, 58

P

pain, 37
paradigm, 132
parietal lobe, 33
pathways, 38
pattern, 46
perceive, 41
Perceived control, 85
percept, 46
perception, 21, 50
Perception, 43
physical states, 48
physically, 99
Physiological, 59
physiological state, 89
Plato, 48
pleasurable, 34
pomodoro, 130
posture, 27, 90
pragmatic, 121
prayer, 133
Pride, 65
procrastination, 124
Proprioception, 19
psychoactive drugs, 50
Psychological needs, 61
psychologically, 50

punishment, 35
pupil, 42

R

rage, 37
RAS, 56
rational thought, 121
Reappraisal, 71
Recognize, 125
rehabilitation, 39
Reinforce, 121
release, 136
release and let go, 136
REM, 74
res cogitans, 48
res extensa, 48
respiration, 36
response, 120
Response, 66, 67
Response modulation, 72
restlessness, 54
reticular activating system, 56
retreat, 137
reward, 35
rewired, 39
Rubin's Vase illusion, 46
Rumination, 69

S

Sadness, 65
safety, 59
saturation, 43

schedule, 133
script, 124
sedative, 73
Selective attention, 44
self limiting beliefs, 94
Self-actualization, 59
self-aware, 62
self-concept, 77
self-esteem, 78
self-ideal, 78
self-image, 77
Self-Perception Theory, 76
Self-regulation, 63
Sensation, 21
sensations, 43
sensorimotor, 30
sensory receptors, 22
Serotonin, 53
sexuality, 37
Shame, 65
sight, 21
signaling, 76
situation, 120
Situation, 66
Situation modification, 68
Situation selection, 67
Sleep, 74
sluggish, 93
smell, 21
social information, 86
Social signals, 76
sound, 21
spinal cord, 30
stance, 90

stimulants, 134
stimuli, 46
stimulus, 19, 120
stress, 53
Stress, 54, 79
stressor, 55
Stressors, 80
subliminal, 50
substantia nigra, 28
Surprise, 65
surrender, 137
survival, 115
symptoms, 103
synapses, 52
systematic, 125

T

Task needs, 61
taste, 21
temporal lobe, 33
tension, 109
thalamus, 28
the endocrine system, 34
therapeutic, 39
thinking, 48
Thought suppression, 70
thoughts, 64
touch, 21
transformation, 16
triad, 120
trifecta, 120
trigger, 99

U

unconscious, 36, 40, 44
unconsciously, 44
Unconsciousness, 21

V

value, 120
values, 118
Ventral, 28

vestibular, 21
vibrations, 19
vigilance, 54
vision, 41

W

William James, 49
working memory, 52
Worry, 70

www.ingramcontent.com/pod-product-compliance
Lightning Source LLC
Chambersburg PA
CBHW070849050426
42453CB00012B/2108